BLACKSTONE'S SECRETS OF MAGIC

Harry Blackstone

Here a world-famous magician reveals some of his most baffling secrets. Over 100,000 copies of this collection are now in print.

More than 100 tricks are clearly explained and illustrated in this collection, from a simple sleight of hand that produces a cigarette out of thin air to the more elaborate stage presentations such as the "Disappearing Woman." There is a valuable section on mental telepathy and "other world" effects, as well as a careful explanation of how to present magic to its best advantage through the dec technique of misdirection. For it i the proper use of misdirection th simplest trick becomes a mystery.

Magic is a fascinating and enjc art — for the magician as well as foɪ ɪɪɪ baffled onlookers. Now completely revised and brought up to date, BLACKSTONE'S SECRETS OF MAGIC is a book that provides suspense and excitement with every page.

BLACKSTONE'S SECRETS OF MAGIC

by
Harry
Blackstone

NEW, REVISED EDITION

Melvin Powers
Wilshire Book Company

12015 Sherman Road, No. Hollywood, CA 91605

Library of Congress Catalog Card Number 58–6630
Copyright © 1929, 1958
By Doubleday & Company, Inc.
Printed in the United States of America
All Rights Reserved

Published by arrangement with Doubleday & Company, Inc.

ISBN 0-87980-260-X

Contents

III   *The "Linking Rings" and the "Cups and Balls"*

IV   *Mental Mysteries and Spirit Tricks*

Contents

V Stage Magic and Illusions

VI Selected Secrets

How to Present Magic

THE presentation of magic is a distinct art in itself. It is different from any other form of public appearance, yet it has certain points in common with many of them.

The impromptu magician must be an extemporaneous speaker; the comedy magician must be a comedian; the platform magician must be something of a lecturer; and the stage magician must certainly be an actor. Yet this is a good rule that does not work both ways. The best speakers, comedians, lecturers and actors may not be capable of becoming good magicians.

Why? Because there is an important element of psychology in the presentation of magic—something which the magician learns partly by instinct, and largely by experience.

There are many difficulties which confront the magician. He must always do two things at once—perform an effect for his audience and operate a trick for himself. He is telling one story and thinking another. A slip will injure his prestige; and if he slips he will never receive sympathy, but will be the object of ridicule.

To offset these difficulties, the magician has a tremendous power in his behalf. It is a simple application of the rule that "you can't beat a man at his own game." The magician is playing a game with his audience; he knows the game and the audience does not.

Therein lies the charm of magic—the lure that brings thousands to the art. Because of it, a mediocre performer, weak as a speaker and devoid of dramatic ability may thoroughly mystify a group of highly intelligent people. Yet in that strength lies weakness. Encouraged by the ease with which they can mystify, many budding performers are neglectful of presentation.

The magic of 1960 has one flaw. Too many observers attribute its marvels to the device, rather than the deceptionist. In this Atomic Age, "push-button" magic has come into the ascendant and it is something strictly to be shunned. No matter how well a trick works, it must bear the stamp of the individual who performs it, not the manufacturer who supplied it.

For that reason tricks with hidden "gimmicks" are coming into their own. They give the magician the benefit of mechanical devices without the audience recognizing it. Inventive genius is important to magic, which is all the more reason why it should be kept secret. This conforms to the fundamental principle of the magician's art, namely:

MISDIRECTION: This is an application of the law of suggestion, patterned particularly to the magician's purpose. It is a psychological fact that a person's interest can be focused upon only one thing at a time; that to divide attention is to lose it.

The magician takes advantage of this in his work. He carries attention one way so that people will forget the other. The simple example is the pretended placement of a coin (or other object) in the left hand while actually palming or retaining it in the right.

Inexperienced magicians become self-conscious and exaggerate such actions as though the moves should be watched closely. Actually, sleights should be performed with a nonchalance whenever possible. The more natural the manner, the greater the deception.

In picking up a wand or some other object, the magician may dispose of something that he has already palmed, again utilizing misdirection. In many of the tricks that appear in this book, certain routines or suggestions are given as part of the misdirection essential to those effects.

STYLE: A performer's style of presentation not only aids in misdirection but types him in the minds of the audience. To perform out of character is a mistake, and in recent years we have seen the development of many new and unusual magical effects suited to individual styles.

For example, the so-called "sucker" tricks, which apparently go wrong and then turn out right, are excellently suited to the beginner or the casual performer who treats his legerdemain in light or humorous style. Today magic has become an adjunct to a master of ceremonies, comedians, or even public speakers, and with the rise of television the art has entered a new era.

Over TV attention can be focused upon close-up effects as well as large stage illusions. During the presentation of big effects the viewers can be taken on stage, so to speak, making every spectator the equivalent of a committee member from the audience. This is helpful, giving magic a greater impact, but it has changed the current style.

The really modern magician must be his natural self or adopt a humorous style, rather than play an outright mysterioso. The old-line prestidigitator, who used the footlights as a chalk-line barrier between himself and his audience, has gone the way of the witch doctor and the medicine man.

Not that such presentation is totally outmoded. On the contrary, it has a dramatic quality when judiciously applied. But the magician who favors the mysterious style must rise to it when occasion calls, rather than adopt it as his one and only pose.

Magic today should be geared to modern speed. Audiences become bored with the poseur or raconteur who wastes time trying to prove how good he is by using words when a few tricks would be better. One of the smash effects in the repertoire of a highly successful magician of the new school takes him exactly three seconds to present. Then he has gone on with something else, while the audience is still catching its breath.

THE PROGRAM: The preceding comments have emphasized the importance of choosing a proper program, that is, picking the right tricks for the right occasion. It is of primary importance that the budding magician should try to be different.

If every magician is cutting up a rope and restoring it, the best plan is to cut out ropes entirely. Even when a magician has invented a good trick of his own he can often afford to drop it when everyone else starts imitating it, and invent something else.

It may not have to be better, because no trick is good when it becomes commonplace. That is why basic magic is somewhat cyclic. Great tricks go into oblivion, only to rise to new favor, sometimes in fresh guise.

In choosing a program, one factor should be kept in mind: the audience. They are the folk who must be amused, mystified, and, above all, entertained. So set your pace to please them.

For close range, pocket tricks are best. Use as many ordinary objects as you can. When special apparatus is involved, employ only items that may be passed for examination. For platform or stage, larger equipment is required, scaling in size according to the scope of the show.

Here the essential thing to remember is that you are working for a group, rather than for individuals who inject their own notions or challenges into the more intimate close-up show. But above all:

The one way to learn magic is to begin doing it. It is one art in which experience is the best teacher. Those words are as true today as when the first introduction to *Secrets of Magic* was penned, nearly thirty years ago.

Biographical Note

FOR half a century the name Blackstone has symbolized magic in the minds of the American public. Today thousands of magic enthusiasts date their interest in the mystic art from the time they first saw Blackstone on the stage. This is indeed appropriate, for Harry Blackstone himself gained his inspiration when he witnessed a performance by the Great Kellar at McVicker's Theatre in Chicago.

After rising to a headliner in the days of vaudeville, Blackstone expanded his show to full evening proportions, and during World War II he toured the military bases with a complete magical extravaganza requiring a company of more than thirty persons. In subsequent years he played all the leading theaters of the United States and Canada, from coast to coast, with his "Show of 1001 Wonders."

The thousand-and-first wonder was Blackstone himself, the white-haired wizard who can perform every type of magic from deft, close-up sleights with cards to sawing a girl in half with an electric buzz-saw, yet restoring her without a scratch. It was such versatility that won Blackstone the rating of "America's Number-One Magician"—a title which he still retains.

Esteemed by fellow members of his craft, Blackstone was elected president of the Magicians' Guild of America and has contributed greatly to the success of that organization. Today still another generation is witnessing Blackstone's magic through the medium of television, as the maestro of mystery is featured on many TV programs.

WALTER B. GIBSON

Blackstone's
Secrets
of
Magic

CHAPTER ONE

Effective Pocket Tricks

POCKET magic has become an art in itself. Years ago they had no place in the magician's repertoire. There were only a few worth-while tricks that could be shown in an impromptu manner.

But the demand for this style of entertainment has greatly increased; and quite as much attention has been given to the devising of clever little mysteries as has been devoted to the invention of stage effects.

There are some very clever tricks of this nature that require no apparatus whatever; but others need special appliances of a miniature nature—articles which can be carried in the pocket and given for inspection whenever required.

In this section I have made no division between the two types. My whole purpose has been to explain the most effective pocket tricks, giving exact instructions as to their working. Most of the special appliances may be obtained from reliable dealers in magical apparatus; others can be easily prepared. But it should be remembered that all magical apparatus should be carefully constructed, and this is particularly true of special pocket tricks which may be subjected to close inspection.

1. TORN AND RESTORED PAPER

The trick of tearing a piece of paper and restoring it to its original condition is one that has been performed for many years, and which has been presented in a variety of ways. In most instances, two sheets of paper are used, one being substituted for the other during the course of the trick.

The method which I shall explain here is not a new one; but it has come into recent popularity, because it disposes of the extra piece of paper in a most ingenious manner.

The effect of the trick is as follows: The magician shows a strip of thin paper, and tears it into pieces. He has shown his hands absolutely empty; and when he folds up the torn pieces, he keeps them constantly in sight.

But when the papers are unfolded, they are restored into a single strip!

The trick must be performed with a special crepe paper, which may be purchased in narrow rolls at stationery stores. This paper can be stretched to twice its length.

The magician begins with a single sheet of paper, about twelve inches long—only about an inch in width. He tears it deliberately in half; then he tears it some more; but he only tears one section of the paper. The result is that he has a six inch strip remaining when he folds the torn pieces.

He holds this in his left hand, calling attention to the fact that the end of the paper is always in view. With his right hand he draws the paper slowly between his left thumb and forefinger, exerting pressure so that the paper stretches as it emerges.

The result is that he draws forth a twelve inch strip of paper—presumably the piece with which he began—but in reality, half of the original strip!

The "getaway" or disposal of the torn pieces is an important item. Inasmuch as only one strip is used, there is little suspicion of remaining pieces. If the performer is near a table or a chair, he can easily drop them (folded tightly) on the floor.

In the open, the best plan is to show the right hand empty, and to moisten the fingers every now and then while drawing out the restored strip. While doing this, the right thumb and fingers take hold of the extra pieces and leave them in the mouth during the second or third moistening process. The tongue pushes the paper up in the cheek.

Another plan is to tear off a corner of the original strip, and to keep that corner in view all the time. After the paper is folded, it is transferred from the right hand to the left; but the extra pieces are kept in the right.

As the left hand shows the complete piece folded up, with the corner still in view, the right hand has plenty of opportunity to pocket the extra pieces without suspicion.

A clever plan is to use a ruler to show the approximate length of the paper. Put the ruler in the pocket. Show the hands empty and proceed. As the paper is drawn out in one hand, the other reaches in the pocket for the ruler, leaving the extra pieces there.

Both measurements should be made quickly, as it is likely that the paper will vary slightly before and after the restoration.

2. ANOTHER PAPER TEARING

This is a variation of the trick just described.

The effect is exactly the same; and the method is quite similar; but instead of crepe paper, very thin tissue is used.

A strip of this paper is folded in half at the center, and a few light dabs of paste are applied to make it appear as a single strip of ordinary thickness. Pressed flat, this strip will pass as a single layer.

It is torn in half. The portion with the fold at the end is kept intact, but the other half is torn several times. The doubled piece is then separated by pressure of the fingers, and is drawn out as a single strip—the exact length of the original double strip.

The torn pieces are disposed of by any of the methods previously described.

In tearing the paper in either one of these tricks, it is not difficult to make the spectators believe that the paper is being torn indiscriminately. The magician should make a great show of the torn ends, and the smaller fragments.

3. THE BALL AND TUBE

The magician exhibits a tiny tube of brass, slightly over an inch in height and about five-eighths of an inch in diameter. In addition, he has a solid steel ball, which may be set upon the tube.

He holds the tube upright in his left hand, with the ball on top, and mentions that both objects are made of solid metal; nevertheless the steel will show its power over brass.

The "Ball and Tube" showing the secret removal of the outer tube.

"You can imagine," he remarks, "that the ball is growing smaller —or that the tube is unable to withstand its weight. See—it is gradually sinking into the tube."

The spectators are doubtful at first; but as they watch, they see the ball sink bit by bit until its top alone is visible.

"A little squeeze on the side of the tube," says the magician; "and the ball will emerge."

He squeezes the tube with his right thumb and forefinger, and little by little the ball comes out. It hesitates at the finish, but another squeeze and it rests on top of the tube. Both the ball and the tube are immediately given for examination.

Two tubes are used in the trick. One fits easily over the other. Both are made of thin brass, and they can be exhibited as a single tube, before the trick.

The inside diameter of the outer tube is virtually the same as the outside diameter of the inner tube. The ball has the same diameter—five-eighths of an inch—and it is just large enough to rest on top of the inner tube, and just small enough to drop through the outer tube.

The tubes are held as one at the finger tips of the left hand, and the ball is placed on top. The four fingers and the thumb form a cluster about the bottom of the tubes. When pressure is slightly released, the ball will sink, pushing the inner tube down with it. The fingers prevent the tube from sinking too rapidly.

To make the ball emerge, the fingers must support the bottom of the inner tube, while the thumb draws down the outer tube. The right thumb and forefinger squeeze the tube as though to help the process. This is done with a purpose.

When the ball has reached the top, the right hand covers the tube for an instant to give it another squeeze. The fingers come in front, but the top of the ball is visible above the temporary screen. The right thumb and forefinger grip the outer tube, and draw it straight upward, over the ball. This leaves the inner tube alone with the ball on top, while the extra tube is secretly held in the right hand.

Some performers make the final squeeze at the base of the thumb and forefinger. This is particularly good if the performer is smoking while performing the trick, as his fingers will be free to handle his cigar or cigarette; and this action of the right hand seems so natural that no one will suspect it of holding anything concealed.

In the simplest and newest "getaway," the right hand sets both tubes upon the table—the ball upon them. In moving away the right fingers deliberately draw off the outer tube. Fingers should be pointing directly downward.

In causing the ball to sink and rise, an excellent plan is to insert the tip of the thumb in the bottom of the tube. The lowering and raising of the thumb does the trick, while the fingers support the outer tube.

4. IMPROVED BALL AND TUBE

In this version of the "Ball and Tube" a much larger ball and tube are used. The effect of the trick is precisely the same. The outer tube, however, is of different mechanical construction. It is shorter than the inner tube—a fact which is not noticed as only the upper portion of the tube is in view, the lower part being hidden in the hand.

A loop of strong thread passes through a hole in the lower part of the outer tube, and this is fastened to a piece of cord-elastic that goes under the coat, and through the belt loops of the trousers. A device such as this is known as a "pull."

The trick is done at a slight distance. When the ball has risen, the right hand approaches to take the tube. It pushes the outer tube down and lifts out the inner tube with the ball on top.

The outer tube is momentarily concealed in the left hand, but as all attention is centered on the right, the extra tube is released, and it flies unseen, beneath the coat.

5. BALL AND GLASS TUBE

This is an ingenious variation of the "Ball and Tube." It cannot be done quite as close as the other method—yet the spectators will see more action.

The whole procedure is exactly the same as the first method of the "Ball and Tube," but the tubes are made of glass instead of brass. As a result it is possible to see the ball when it has sunk into the tube.

As the glass is thicker than metal, a little distance is required to make the trick effective, especially as the upper edge of the inner tube is visible. Yet a few feet away, this rim cannot be detected, against the silvery surface of the ball, and the trick is very mysterious in appearance. An amber-tinted glass is best to use.

6. GIANT MATCH PRODUCTION

A very surprising trick.

The magician takes a match-box from his pocket, opens it and extracts a match. But the match is nine inches in length and of proportionate thickness!

The box must be prepared beforehand. It is an ordinary safety-match box; but the inner end of the drawer is cut away, and a V shaped space is made in the bottom of the cover, running from the end toward the center.

The giant match is up the left sleeve.

The right hand places the box in the left, and moving toward the wrist, grasps the end of the match and draws it forward. The drawer of the box is opened, and the right hand slides the box back into the left hand so that the end of the giant match comes inside. Then reaching into the box, he draws the match directly through.

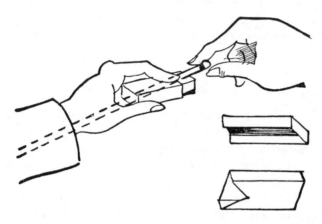

Instead of a dummy match, a match with a metal head may be used. A hole in the metal head enables the performer to insert the head of a small match, and to strike it on the box, after the production of the large match. Whenever the trick is to be done, the head is prepared.

It is also possible to obtain giant safety matches by the box. One of these can be used for the production instead of an imitation.

7. THE CIGARETTE FROM NOWHERE

The magician pretends to roll an imaginary cigarette, going through all the motions of using tobacco, and paper. He places the invisible cigarette in his mouth; strikes a match, and to the surprise of everyone he is smoking a real cigarette.

The whole secret lies in a specially constructed match-box. The drawer of the box is faked by running a metal tube through it, lengthwise at one side. The box is filled with matches and is partly opened; then a cigarette is concealed in the tube.

Everything is pantomime until the performer needs a match. Then he picks up the half opened box, removes a match, and strikes it. As he holds it in his right hand, the left retains the box. Both hands are raised to the mouth, as though lighting a cigarette in the wind. The left hand pushes the drawer of the box shut; this causes the cigarette to project; and it is gripped by the lips.

While the hands still hide the action, the match is used to light the cigarette.

8. IMPROVED CIGARETTE FROM NOWHERE

This is a newer trick than the one just explained; and it has un-usual novelty. The magician shakes a little tobacco from a ten cent bag; throws the grains from hand to hand, and lights a match. Raising the match to his mouth, he withdraws his hands to reveal a lighted cigarette.

The trick lies in the tobacco bag. The bottom is reinforced with metal, and a metal tube extends upward. It holds the cigarette. But when one thumb is kept over the hole in the bottom of the bag, it appears quite normal.

A little tobacco is shaken from the bag, the right hand doing the work, and the thumb keeping the cigarette in place. Then the bag is transferred to the left hand, which has its fingers pointing directly up. The cigarette slides down into the left hand.

The right hand and teeth are used to pull the strings of the bag, which is placed in the pocket by the right hand. The tobacco is poured from the left to the right hand and back again; very little is used, and most of this is dropped during the pouring. The left hand retains the cigarette.

The right strikes a match; the hands are raised, and the lips take the cigarette from the left hand, while the match is used to light it.

9. THE FOUR COLORS

There are many divination tricks, and this one belongs to the list. But it involves a new principle, which has been employed in several similar tricks.

A small circular mirror is used. The back is painted white, and is covered with glass; and on its surface appear four spots of different colors.

The device is laid on the table, and a person is told to cover any one of the spots with a dime. The magician turns his back while this takes place.

When the dime has been removed, the magician picks up the mirror, and turns aside a moment. He finally looks into the reflecting side, and immediately names the color of the spot that was covered.

The method is very ingenious. The surface on which the spots appear has been coated with luminous paint. The paint absorbs light, and when a coin is placed over one of the spots and allowed to remain there about a minute, it leaves a shadow.

When the magician takes the mirror, he slips it under his coat as he turns away from the light, and detects the shadow in the darkness—for the rest of the surface will glow. Thus he knows which spot was covered.

The magician may stay out of the room during the trick and ask that the mirror be passed to him. This proves that he is not in collusion with anyone in the room, and it gives him an opportunity to hold the mirror in darkness.

10. THE DIVINING DIE

This appliance is very simple and inexpensive. A single die about an inch in diameter, and a cubical celluloid box with tight fitting cover.

Someone drops the die in the box; notes the number on top

and puts on the cover. The magician takes the box, holds it to his forehead, and names the top number.

The bottom of the box is quite thin. The sides and top are ornamental; but the smooth bottom is transparent when the die rests against it. Thus if someone turns the box upside down and looks at the bottom, he cannot see through. But when the magician holds the box upright and tilts it slowly forward, he will see the number on the bottom while the die still rests there.

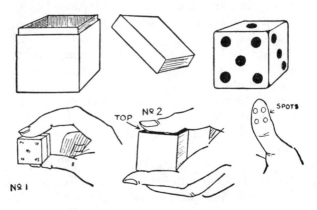

The bottom number tells him the top; for the opposite sides of a die always total seven, and a simple subtraction tells him the top side.

By **way** of variation the magician may hold the box behind his back. In this case he lifts the cover and presses his thumb firmly against the top of the die, replacing the cover immediately.

He hands the box back to someone, and turns his back for an instant. On the ball of his thumb he will see a clear imprint of the upper side of the die with the correct number of spots.

In this form, the trick can be worked with any box, or a die may be placed upright on the palm of the left hand, held behind the back.

11. KNIFE THROUGH THE HANDKERCHIEF

This is another trick with an improvement; both methods will be described under one heading.

The magician borrows a pen-knife and a handkerchief. The handkerchief is spread out and the corners are held by spectators. A square sheet of paper—smaller than the handkerchief—is placed upon the cloth. Then the magician lowers the knife under

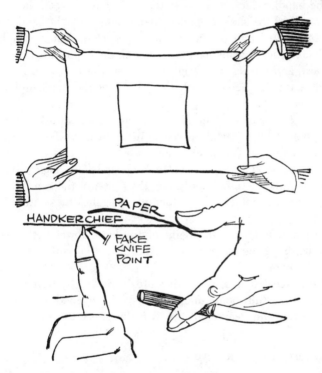

the handkerchief, and states that he will try to cut the paper without injuring the handkerchief—something that appears impossible.

He taps the handkerchief several times, causing the paper to bob up and down. Suddenly he pulls the knife right through the paper—yet the handkerchief is uninjured!

This is all done during the preliminary part of the trick. As he taps the paper through the handkerchief, the magician holds the knife in his right hand. As if by accident, he knocks the paper to the edge of the handkerchief. There the left hand takes the side of the paper—thumb above and fingers beneath. The right hand has moved over also and the left fingers grip the handle of the knife.

The left hand lifts the paper and drops it back on the center of the handkerchief; and it lets the knife fall between the handkerchief and the sheet of paper. Meanwhile the right hand keeps tapping the bottom of the handkerchief as though it still held the knife. Then it grips the knife through the cloth; tilts the blade upward, and pushes it through the paper, the left hand helping.

The paper is pierced with the knife—yet the handkerchief is uninjured.

In the improvement, the magician has the end of a knife blade or a pointed bit of metal hidden in his right hand. He places the paper on the handkerchief; then withdraws it and deliberately exchanges the knife from hand to hand under the paper. But he instantly puts the right hand under the center of the handkerchief and pushes the point of the hidden blade against the center of the cloth.

He lets people feel the point of the knife through the cloth. Then he drops the paper upon it, and the actual knife goes along with the paper.

The concealment of the dull knife blade in the right hand is not at all difficult. Some magicians have it attached to an elastic that runs up the sleeve, but this is really unnecessary.

12. THROUGH THE COAT

This is an effective variation of the previous trick. The magician removes his coat and lays it over the back of an open-backed chair, the back of the coat being toward the audience.

His right hand holds a knife and lowers it behind the coat, while the left hand holds a sheet of paper in front of the coat.

Suddenly the sheet of paper is pierced by the knife, which makes its appearance through the uninjured coat.

The magician simply drops the knife in the collar of the coat as he lowers his right hand. While the right forefinger taps against the center of the coat to indicate the presence of the knife, the left hand raises the paper to show the center of the coat. The left thumb and forefinger are behind the sheet of paper and they pick up the knife, carrying it under the paper to the center of the coat in front. Then the right hand grips the knife through the coat and the left hand pulls the knife through the paper.

With an extra knife blade, the right hand can show the actual point of the knife at the center of the coat, when the left hand lifts the paper. The extra blade may be easily dropped in the inside coat pocket.

13. SELF RISING MATCH-BOX

The match-box that rises and falls on the back of the hand is a rather crude and simple trick. But this method, which the author

has found effective, while involving nothing but the box, makes a new trick.

The match-box is laid *across* the fingers of the left hand. Suddenly it rises—very slowly; then it sinks again. It is finally handed for examination.

The Method: Open the box very slightly in an inward direction. Set that end of the box upon the third finger of the left hand. Close the box with the right hand, catching a very tiny bit of flesh on the left finger.

Now the slightest tipping of the hand will control the box. Even the natural shaking of the fingers is sufficient. With a little practice the performer can make the box rise and fall at will, with no unnatural motion of the left hand.

The right hand in taking the box opens it slightly so it can be removed from the left fingers. People may watch as closely as they desire; yet the magician makes the box obey every command without detection.

14. THE CIGARETTE TUBE

This is one of the finest pocket tricks ever made. The magician is smoking a cigarette. He places it, lighted end downward, in a nickel-plated tube just large enough to receive it; and he places the cover on the tube.

Someone holds the tube. When the cover is removed, the cigarette has completely disappeared.

The cigarette is made of metal, painted white, with a slight tip of brass which is kept between the lips. The tube is open at the inner end; but the outer end has a pierced disc of brass against which a small portion of a genuine cigarette is inserted.

The cigarette may be smoked, for a short while, and it appears to be quite ordinary. When it is pushed into the tube, it fits snugly, and its presence cannot be detected. In fact, if the tube is correctly manufactured, the cigarette can only be removed by jamming a pointed lead pencil into the tube, and pulling it out again.

A special rod is also made that screws into the metal disc and brings out the cigarette.

Some performers vanish a match and cause it to appear in the tube in place of the cigarette. This is simple enough, because a duplicate match is kept inside the fake cigarette. But this part of the trick is hardly worth while. The reproduction of the lighted cigarette is a good effect, however. It is accomplished by the aid of the apparatus shown below.

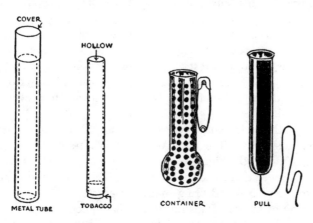

15. THE CIGARETTE HOLDER

The "Cigarette Holder" is a device of metal with airholes all around. It holds a lighted cigarette, and may be carried in the pocket with no fear of burning.

After disappearing the cigarette with the "Cigarette Tube," the magician merely reaches in his pocket and brings out the lighted cigarette.

The best holders are fairly large; they are made of a heavy wire screen, with two clips at the top to hold the cigarette in position, so the lighted end does not touch the bottom of the tube. Some holders have safety pins attached to fasten them in the pocket; but with the larger holder, the size and weight is sufficient.

16. THE MYSTERIOUS CIGARETTE

This combination of cigarette effects is highly effective; following the "Cigarette Tube and Holder" it is unusually good, as the preliminary trick leads up to it.

The magician vanishes a cigarette and reproduces it lighted from his pocket. Again it vanishes and is brought from another pocket. The magician smokes the cigarette; then pushes it, lighted end first, into his collar, where he leaves it resting against his neck!

The first movement is to toss the lighted cigarette from hand to hand. It is dropped from hand to hand with the semblance of a toss, and is allowed to rest across the fingers. The lighted end is toward the little finger, and is allowed to project slightly from the hand; but the little fingers may be bent backward to prevent any contact.

Finally the right hand retains the cigarette by bending in all fingers except the little one. At the same instant the magician pretends to toss the cigarette into the left hand. The left hand is quickly opened and the cigarette is gone. The right hand instantly goes to the pocket and brings out the cigarette.

This bit of by-play leads up to the final effect.

Under his coat the magician has a "Cigarette Pull," a tube of metal with cord elastic attached, which runs through the belt loops of the trousers. In his right coat pocket he has an imitation lighted cigarette—of the type sold very cheaply at novelty stores.

He puffs on the cigarette and takes it in his right hand, while his left gets hold of the "pull." The magician retains a large quantity of smoke in his mouth. He deliberately inserts the lighted end of the cigarette into his left fist, where it goes into the "pull." He releases the "pull" and shows his left hand empty.

His right hand then goes to the pocket and produces the imitation cigarette. He puts it in his mouth and exhales the smoke that is there. By short puffs he appears to smoke the cigarette. Everyone is sure it is a genuine cigarette—and when the magician inserts the supposedly lighted end beneath his collar, everyone will be amazed.

As a follow-up, the "cigarette" can be pushed completely out of sight beneath the collar, and a real lighted cigarette be reproduced from a holder under the cuff of the trousers. A holder located there must be pinned in place.

17. THE DIVINING DIAL

This little device is about the same size as the mirror used in the "Four Color" trick. It consists of a dial with an arrow in the center; and anyone may point the arrow to any spot he wishes. Instead of clock numbers, the dial has eight colored spots as illustrated.

A cover is placed on the little box that contains the dial; and the magician merely sets the whole affair on the table; yet he instantly names the color to which the arrow is pointing.

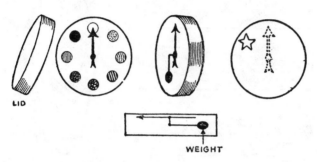

Between the dial and the bottom of the shallow box is a small weight that moves with the pointer. On the bottom of the box (outside) is an ornamental star that seems to have no special purpose; but it indicates the position of one of the colors.

The magician stands the box on its side, and being circular it rolls as he moves his hand along. It stops when the weight is at the bottom. The position of the star on the box then indicates the color to which the arrow is pointing, as the magician has familiarized himself with the dial.

18. THE MUMMY CASE

Various divinations can be performed through the use of weights. One of the adaptions of that principle is the "Mummy Case."

This case is only a few inches long; and it is painted to represent the coffin of an Egyptian mummy. The lid pivots, and spectators are invited to place one of three mummies in the case—hiding the other two.

Each mummy is different in color and appearance; and the performer can instantly name the one that occupies the case, without even touching the little box.

One mummy is weighted in the feet; another in the head. The weight of the third is evenly distributed. The bottom of the box is curved, so the ends do not touch the table.

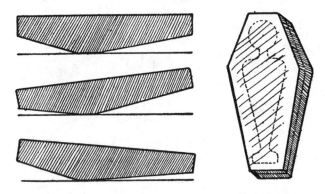

Thus the box will tilt in one direction or the other—or will remain level, according to the particular mummy which is within. This is not noticeable to the average person; but the magician looks for the tilt.

The case should be so constructed that the mummies will fit only one way—thus preventing anyone from reversing one of them.

19. THE FOUR COLOR BLOCKS

Among the newest divination tricks, the "Four Color Blocks" is a novelty. These blocks fit in a shallow box about six inches in length.

Each block has a different color on its opposite sides—the blocks being quite thin, an inch square but only a quarter-inch in thickness. Thus there are eight possible colors; and spectators are requested to arrange the blocks in a row so that any four colors may be in view. Then the box is closed and fastened.

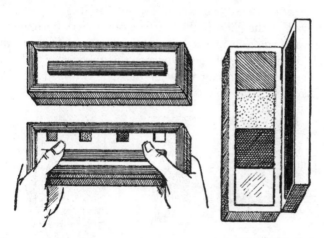

The magician holds the box to his forehead, and immediately names the colors on the tops of the blocks, in their proper order.

The top of the box is paneled, having a raised surface in the center. The magician places his thumbs upon this and presses toward the front of the box. The panel slides and four small openings come into view—one for each block. He notes the colors in an instant, and when he releases pressure, a spring forces the panel back into position.

The box will stand considerable examination, as the panel must be pressed quite firmly to operate. The mechanism is so ingenious that no one will suspect it, especially as the operation cannot be noticed.

20. PENCIL THROUGH COIN

This trick requires a special slide made to hold a coin of half-dollar size. For a reason which will be explained, a "palming coin" of odd design is used instead of a half dollar.

The coin is put in the slide and it can be seen through a hole below the center of the slide. Then a silk handkerchief is put over the slide and a pencil is used to push the handkerchief down through the hole—and completely through the coin!

The trick is a clever one, when properly handled.

One wall of the slide is thicker than the other. It contains a thin piece of metal which represents the center of the coin that is used. By tilting the slide downward, this fake piece will slide into view; but it will disappear when the slide is tipped the other way. That is why the hole is below the center of the slide.

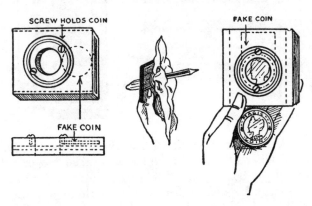

The brass molding which surrounds the round hole may be turned by pressing the fingernail against one of the screws. It shifts less than an inch; but the upper screw may thus be shifted so as to hold the fake metal disc in concealment.

In performing, the slide is set with the fake hidden and locked in place. While the coin is being examined, the magician releases the fake but holds the slide level so that the fake does not appear.

He inserts the coin in the slide, and shows both sides. This lets him drop the fake behind the coin; so when he turns the slide around again, the fake is seen instead of the coin; and he permits the coin to drop out the bottom of the slide, into his hand.

The process of penetration is the easiest part of the trick. By tilting the slide, the magician can push the handkerchief through with the pencil. Just as the handkerchief finishes its journey, he tilts the slide the other way and the fake slides into view.

The important part of the trick is getting the real coin back into the slide at the finish.

The magician removes the handkerchief and boldly shows the slide with the fake in view. Then he lays it on the fingers of his right hand—the exact spot where he has retained the real coin.

Thus the slide covers the real coin. The hand is flat—palm upward. The top of the slide is toward the performer.

He tilts his hand toward himself. The fake slides back into its hiding place. He releases the coin at the same instant, and it drops from his right hand to his left. But the keenest observer will be positive it dropped from the slide.

The right hand now has the slide out of view; and the right thumb secretly pushes the screw that holds the fake in place. The slide itself may then be given for inspection, along with the coin.

21. THE COLORED BARS

This is another divination trick. Three cylindrical bars, each one inch in length are used. The bars are painted different colors.

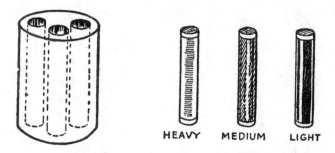

HEAVY   MEDIUM   LIGHT

The magician shows a cylindrical box slightly deeper than the length of the bars. It has three holes in the top, and they are numbered 1, 2, and 3.

He holds the box behind his back and lets some person drop the bars in—the first bar in hole 1; next in hole 2; the third in hole 3.

Then the magician immediately names the color of the bar in

each hole. And he is always correct, no matter how often the trick may be repeated.

Why? Because each bar is of different weight. One, for example, may be made of lead; another of copper; the third of aluminum. Such great difference of weight is not, however, essential; and all the bars may be made of the same material, but hollowed in different proportions.

The bottom of the box is just a thin disc of metal; and the performer's finger, resting there, can feel the difference in the weight of each bar as it drops.

22. THE RED HOT BALL

While hardly a pocket trick, this is an unusual mystery for the parlor—or for any close-up performance. A brass ball some two and a half inches in diameter is used. It rests on a little stand; and taking it from there, the magician passes it for inspection, stating that he will perform a trick with it.

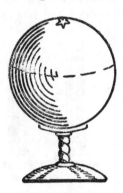 

SULPHURIC ACID

QUICK LIME

A spectator holds the ball, and it seems warm to him. Then it becomes hot; and finally he is forced to drop it on the floor. Anyone who tries to pick it up will give up the attempt.

The ball is hollow; and it screws apart in the center. On one hemisphere is a little cylinder. This is filled beforehand with sulphuric acid; while quicklime is placed around it. Then the top is screwed on the ball.

A star on top indicates how the ball should be set, to prevent its contents from mixing. That is why a little stand is used.

When the spectators begin to examine the ball, they naturally turn it over, causing the sulphuric acid to join the quicklime. The ball will become hot very quickly.

23. CIGARETTE TO CIGAR

This is a good trick for the smoker. He lights a cigarette; then pushes it into his left fist; and it turns to a cigar, which he continues to smoke as though nothing had occurred.

The cigarette is a real one; but the cigar is an imitation made of wood. It is hollow, and of just sufficient length to receive a cigarette. It is held in the left hand; and the cigarette is pushed in—lighted end last.

The cigar has an air passage going to the stem; so the magician can continue to smoke for a minute or so, just as though he had a real cigar.

24. COLORED CRAYONS

Reverting to divination tricks, there is one that requires only a few colored crayons; yet which is quite effective.

The magician receives a colored crayon behind his back, and, still holding it there, faces his audience and points to the person who gave him the crayon.

"You give me a green crayon," he says; and the spectator admits that the magician is correct.

As he turns to face his audience, the magician marks his right thumbnail with the crayon. In pointing to the person, he sees the color on his nail and immediately names it. The color is quickly removed by the forefinger.

25. BLACKSTONE'S PAPER BALL TRICK

This trick has been performed by the author for many years, and it has come to be recognized as one of the best of impromptu tricks. I shall explain it with its many variations.

Three little paper pellets. They are thrown on the table, and two of them are dropped in the left hand. The third is thrown away—but when the left hand is opened, out roll the three paper balls.

Time and again the trick is repeated. Yet the three paper balls constantly appear in the left hand. Every movement is natural and convincing; and when the trick is finished with some of the variations that will be given, the spectators are unanimous in declaring it one of the most perplexing mysteries they have ever witnessed.

While the trick is not difficult, it is one that improves with practice, and the magician who uses it should seek to show it effectively.

A fourth paper ball is used, and it is concealed between the tips of the first and second fingers of the right hand. It is placed there with the aid of the thumb, which holds it against the second finger until the forefinger is ready to take its place.

With the extra ball in position, pick up the first paper ball between the thumb and the tip of the forefinger. You can show the inside of your hand as you do so; for the thumb hides the extra ball. Drop the first paper ball in the left hand.

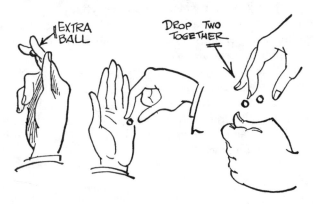

Repeat the movement with the second ball; but in dropping it in the hand, let the extra ball go with it, immediately closing the left hand.

Spread the fingers of the right hand, and pick up the third ball between the thumb and second finger. Pretend to throw it away, but clip it between your finger tips. Roll the three paper balls from the left hand, and you are ready to start again.

By way of variation, reach under the table and pretend to knock the third paper ball up through. Whenever a glass-topped table is available, this makes a remarkable illusion; the left hand, dropping three balls at the same instant, gives the effect that one ball came up through the glass.

Another scheme is to drop the third ball in the pocket—apparently. Always retain it in the right hand.

By way of variation, cup the left hand, and in dropping in the first paper ball, let the extra ball go in. This gives you unusual freedom with the second ball, which follows. Then throw the third away—the three will be in the left hand.

Another surprise is the introduction of some other object, such as a coin or a lump of sugar. Drop the third ball in the pocket, and while rolling out three from the left hand, obtain the other article. Then place two balls in the left hand, without showing the right empty; and let the large object drop in also. Pretend to throw the third ball away, and the coin or lump of sugar will roll from the left hand instead.

Place the two balls in the left hand, and let the extra one fall with them. Put the large object in your pocket, and the three balls again appear in the left hand.

Now comes a vanish of the three paper balls. Put them one by one into the left hand—apparently; but retain each in the right hand, between the fingers. When you pocket the third ball, drop all three in your pocket; and show your left hand empty.

Or place all three apparently in the left hand; then show the left hand empty, at the same time dropping the three from right hand onto the floor. This is specially suited when seated at a table.

Some previous preparation helps the trick. Take some ordinary pins and push them through the cloth under your vest, so that the points are downward. Impale three paper balls on each pin.

After vanishing the paper balls, show the left hand empty; then extend the right hand and show it empty too. At the same time, the left hand goes to the vest and draws off three paper balls.

Everyone wonders where the balls have gone; and when you extend your left hand, they roll on the table again. During the surprise, your right hand captures three from one of the pin points; then the left hand drops the three paper balls in the pocket on the left side, and the right hand rolls the balls on the table.

By retaining one ball in the left hand, you can hold it cupped; then the right hand drops two in the left and throws the third away; the three appear in the left. You are back at the beginning again; and at a later period you can get three more from your vest to conclude the trick.

Of course the routine should not be overdone. At the same time it is one of those tricks that gets better as it progresses; and it should be adapted to the occasion. When to do a trick and how long to do it is something that must be learned by experience.

26. THE UNCANNY DIE

This is a trick with a die that is somewhat different from others. The die is placed upon the magician's palm and is covered with a little metal box of five sides—large enough to fit over the die but with no cover.

One person has noted the upper side of the die—which we will suppose is six. The magician extends his hand to another spectator and asks him to lift the cover and note the side. He sees a three.

A third person sees another number. In fact, no one is sure which side of the die is up after all!

Skill and boldness accomplish the trick, yet it is not overly-difficult. The die is set on the fingers of the left hand. The cover is placed over it and the thumb steadies the cover. As the hand is moved the fingers spread slightly; the die settles between them, and in pressing it up into the cover, the performer gives it a quarter turn.

With a little practice this can be done with no apparent motion. It is indetectible under the very eyes of the observers.

27. THE ADHESIVE CIGARETTE PACK

This is an interesting stunt. The performer attaches an empty cigarette package to the wall by merely pressing a match against it. Then he puts several pencils, a fountain pen and some matches into the pack. Still it stays there and supports them all.

A package of twenty cigarettes is used—and it must be a pack which is enclosed in wax paper. The wax paper is torn off. The empty pack is set against the wood-work of the doorway. A match is lighted, and the burning end is pressed against the side of the package, pressing it firmly against the wood-work. The magician blows out the light before it can ignite the cigarette pack.

The surface of the pack is waxy because of the wax-paper covering. The heat causes the wax to become sticky—instantly—and the pack adheres to the wood-work.

It will stay there quite firmly, and it is surprising how many different articles such as cigars, pencils, etc. can be placed in it without their weight causing it to fall.

28. THE IMPROVED COIN BOX

The box consists of two parts, the bottom (with a flange), and the top. There is no trick to the box.

There are four important phases of this trick.

(A) Balance the bottom of the box on the tip of your left second finger, with the first and third fingers pressing against the sides. A marked half dollar is dropped in the box. Take the cover in the right hand between the thumb and fingers. Hold the cover vertically.

As the right hand reaches the left, tilt up the bottom of the box slightly with your left thumb. Press the inside of the cover against the outer edge of the bottom, and press with the cover. The bottom will swing up to a vertical position, and the cover will lock in the flange that is on the bottom of the box (underneath). Instantly you let the box fall horizontal on your fingers and place the left thumb on top. The bottom of the box is now UPSIDE DOWN. The fine construction of the box makes this move exceptionally easy; the box does not move from its position on the left hand, and the turnover cannot be detected. You can fool yourself with it! The top of the box covers it.

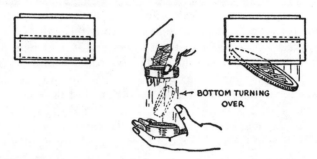

LEFT AND RIGHT: Action of the coin when bottom of box is inverted.
CENTER: Turning the bottom right side up.

(B) Shake the box, pressing down on the cover with the left thumb. The coin will rattle inside the inverted bottom. Now toss the box easily towards the right hand, and swing the right hand up catching the box with the right fingers beneath and the right thumb above. With a little practice you can execute this move without fail, and the box may be tossed from hand to hand two or three times if you wish, but it should end in the right hand.

(C) Hold a playing card in the left hand, fingers beneath, thumb above, the card tilted slightly forward. Swing the right hand towards the left; at the same time tilt up the outer side of the box by pressing on the inner side with the right thumb. The coin will be lying on the right fingers, and as you slide the box on to the card, the coin will go beneath, where it is held by the left fingers. The sweeping move of the right hand, with the back of the hand toward spectators, prevents a "flash" of the coin.

Command the coin to fall through the box and the card. Simply release the coin with the left fingers and it drops on the table.

(D) After penetrating coin, hold box between index finger and thumb. Relax fingers slightly, and at same time touch extreme bottom of box with middle finger and the bottom will drop right side up, into the other hand, which is held beneath.

Then drop the cover and give both sections for examination.

Note: In place of the first movement, this action is effective: set the box on the palm of the left hand. Hold the cover between the thumb and forefinger of the right. The coin is in the box.

As the right hand is lowered so the cover is over the box, the second finger of the right hand presses the front edge of the box. The pressure causes the box to turn over, and the cover is immediately placed upon it.

29. COIN CHANGING SLIDE

A clever mechanical device for exchanging one coin for another or causing the disappearance or appearance of a coin.

The slide is a flat strip of wood, with a circular depression in the

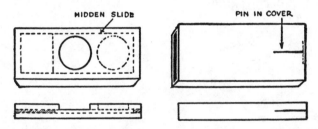

center—large enough to receive a small coin. The slide is pushed into a long cover, open at one end; when the slide is removed, a coin has appeared in the center.

Both the slide and the cover will stand close examination, as the secret is virtually indetectible.

The slide is hollow, with a shorter slide within it. There are two depressions in the inner slide, which may be pushed back or forth so that either comes beneath the outside opening.

The only way to operate the inner slide is by inserting a pin through one of two small holes (one at each end of the slide), according to the direction in which the inner slide is to be pushed.

The inner end of the outer cover is provided with such a pin. It is permanently in place, projecting outward. When the slide is pushed in, the pin enters the hole and shifts the inner slide. The operation is automatic, and the magician may use the ingenious apparatus in whatever manner he may choose.

It is particularly suited for the reproduction of a coin that has disappeared, as in

30. PENNY AND DIME TRICK

The most ingenious of coin tricks. A penny is placed overlapping a dime. When the dime is covered with the penny, it disappears.

The penny is a hollowed-shell. The underside of the dime is faced with the tail side of a penny. The shell penny picks up the dime, and the two form what appears to be an ordinary penny.

This may be made with any two coins where one is slightly larger than the other.

CHAPTER TWO

Magic with Apparatus

A GREAT percentage of magicians are interested in magic with apparatus, as distinguished from pocket tricks and stage illusions. A great many amateurs would rather give regular magical shows than do impromptu magic; and the great bulk of the semiprofessional magicians are necessarily limited to apparatus of small size because they more frequently appear upon the platform than upon the stage.

As for the beginners in magic; most of them look forward to performing before groups rather than individuals, and by choosing the proper tricks with apparatus they can make progress very rapidly.

The tricks which are explained here have been chosen because of their effectiveness, novelty, and reliability; and they will prove useful to all classes of magicians.

1. THE REPEATING HANDKERCHIEF VANISH

Magicians vanish handkerchiefs so frequently that such a demonstration is not unusual. But when a magician makes the same handkerchief vanish again and again, his audience will sit up and take notice.

Yet the repeating handkerchief vanish is merely an adaptation of an old piece of apparatus—the "Handkerchief Pull." This is a cup-shaped appliance attached to a piece of cord elastic. The elastic runs through a safety pin below the arm-hole of the vest, and through the belt loops of the trousers.

When the "pull" is held in the left hand, and a handkerchief is pushed into the fist, the "pull" when released will fly under the coat, so that the hand may be shown empty.

In the repeating vanish, the "pull" has a hole punched in its outer edge. A piece of black thread one foot long is tied through the hole; and the other end is attached to the corner of the handkerchief.

The handkerchief is pushed into the "pull" and the apparatus is left under the coat, ready for use.

In performing, the magician reaches beneath his coat and pulls out the handkerchief, as though taking it from his pocket. He spreads it in front of him, the corner with the thread being at the left.

Then the right hand takes the left corner of the handkerchief and moves it slowly to the right. The left hand rests idly against the coat lapel. The thread becomes taut as the right hand progresses, and then draws the pull outward, so that it may be gripped by the left hand as it reaches the lapel.

The left hand is advanced a trifle, drawing the elastic to its full length. Beginning with the threaded corner, the right hand pokes the handkerchief into the "pull," and the piece of silk disappears.

It is immediately ready for a repetition of the trick.

With the proper "patter" this becomes a very entertaining bit of magic.

"The first trick I ever learned," says the magician, "was with this silk handkerchief that I always carry in my pocket. I found that when I pushed it into my left fist, in this manner, something unexpected would happen. The handkerchief would disappear!

"I learned this trick in school. The teacher asked me what I was doing. I told her that I had merely taken a silk handkerchief from my pocket—like this; had pushed it into my fist—like this; and had made it disappear.

"She sent me home with a note to my father. When he asked me what I had been doing, I told him that I had only taken a silk handkerchief from my pocket in this manner; had held it in my right hand, and pushed it into my left fist, and made it disappear.

"My father called up the neighbors. When they came in, he told me to go ahead, so I took a silk handkerchief from my pocket; held it up for all to see; poked it into my left fist and made it disappear!

"So that's how I became a magician. The first show I ever gave, I began by taking a silk handkerchief from my pocket, holding it in my right hand, and pushing it into my left fist—from which it disappeared.

"And now I will show you my favorite trick. I take a silk handkerchief from my pocket; hold it in my right hand and slowly place it in my left fist—and you see the handkerchief has disappeared."

2. THE DRUM PRODUCTION

This is a very simple yet effective production of a group of silk handkerchiefs. The apparatus consists of a cylinder six or eight inches in diameter, and four or five inches in depth, mounted on a slender rod one-half an inch thick. The cylinder is set on its side, and the rod, which is about a foot in height, is mounted on a large nickel-plated base.

The magician places a piece of tissue paper in front of the cylinder, and fastens it in position with a band of metal. Then he breaks the paper and proceeds to extract a dozen or more silk handkerchiefs from the empty tube.

Paper may be placed over both sides of the cylinder, and some handkerchiefs taken from each side.

The spectators do not suspect where the handkerchiefs come from, because they do not believe that a silk handkerchief one foot square can be passed through a tube only a half-inch thick.

The handkerchiefs are concealed in the base; and they come up the slender rod, which is hollow. The end of each handkerchief is twisted around the one next in line, forming a chain. The first handkerchief should be black—the color of the inside of the cylinder. After the front paper has been fastened on, the magician gets hold of the end of this silk, which is at the top of the rod, and draws it upward. This begins the chain, and the handkerchiefs are produced in quick succession.

A solid base with a hole through the center may be used; in this event the handkerchiefs are compressed in the hollow leg of an undraped table, which has a hole in the top to correspond with the tube above.

3. THE NEW CONFETTI BOWLS

The magician uses two bowls of metal, each six inches in diameter, and four inches in height.

He fills the first bowl with confetti, and places the other mouth to mouth with it. Upon removing the upper bowl, the confetti has doubled in quantity, now filling both bowls.

The confetti is leveled; and the empty bowl is placed upon it. Again the confetti doubles in quantity.

For the third time it is leveled, and the empty bowl placed upon it. Upon removal of the upper bowl, the confetti has doubled again.

The bowls are constructed as follows:

(A) An empty bowl that has a loose lining which fits snugly. The lining is shallower than the bowl; and its inner surface is covered with confetti, which is glued or cemented in place.

(B) A bowl filled with confetti. Near the mouth are four bits of metal that project about a half an inch inward. They are equi-distant apart.

A celluloid disc also fits in the bowl. It has a small knob in the center; and four cut-out portions on the rim to correspond with the arms that project from the sides of the bowl. Both sides of the disc are coated with confetti.

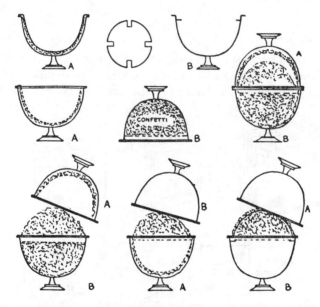

Bowl B is filled with confetti beforehand. Then the celluloid disc is placed in it; the cut-outs are slid over the projecting arms. The knob on the disc is upward, and by turning it, the disc is locked below the arms. Then the bowl may be inverted.

In performing, Bowl A is shown empty. It is filled with confetti. Bowl B is picked up in a careless manner—apparently empty because it is upside down—and is placed on Bowl A.

The bowls are inverted. Bowl A is lifted off (the loose lining with it) and the confetti appears to have doubled.

The confetti is leveled off, and the knob is turned so that the celluloid disc of Bowl B is free.

Bowl A is set on Bowl B; they are inverted. The disc sinks into Bowl A, and the confetti from Bowl B is piled upon it, when Bowl B is lifted.

Now the confetti is leveled off to the disc. Bowl B is placed upon Bowl A. The bowls are inverted. This time Bowl A is lifted free, leaving the lining behind. The interior of the lining gives the appearance of a bowlful of confetti.

4. DIE, FRAME, AND RIBBON

This magical effect is both modern and mysterious.

A square frame, about six inches on a side, is used; also a large block of wood painted to resemble a die. The die fits in the frame.

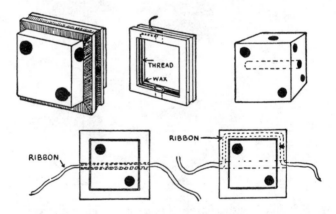

A hole runs through the die and there are corresponding holes in opposite sides of the frame.

The die is placed in the frame, and a ribbon is run through the holes, penetrating both the die and the frame. The ends of the ribbon are held by spectators. There is no possible way to remove the die.

The magician seizes the die and takes it right out of the frame, *leaving the ribbon through the frame.* The die is solid, and everything may be examined!

The inside of the frame is beveled. Therein lies the secret; but there is nothing suspicious about the construction of the frame. Around one of the holes of the frame, on the inside, is a slight coating of wax. A slip-knot of black thread surrounds the hole, being pressed against the wax. The free end of the thread runs around inside the frame, being waxed at the corners, and out the other hole, where it is attached to the outside of the frame by the dab of wax. The thread is not seen.

The die is placed in position, and the ribbon is pushed through the holes. But when the magician pulls the ribbon through, his hand, which is hidden by the die, pulls the thread instead. This yanks the ribbon *around the die* through the beveled depression. As soon as the end of the ribbon emerges, the magician seizes it. In handing the ends to the spectators, he pulls the slip-knot off the end of the ribbon and drops the thread onto the floor. This is easily done.

The die fits rather tightly in the frame, so it does not need the ribbon to support it. It sticks firmly in place. Nothing could appear fairer.

All the magician has to do is to pull out the die or knock it from the frame. The spectators are told to pull on the ribbon, so it immediately runs straight through the frame, the instant that the die is released.

The secret of this excellent trick is known to comparatively few magicians. The apparatus will stand close inspection; and the frame is painted solid black so that the black thread will not show. The author considers it to be one of the best effects of recent years, especially suited to the requirements of the platform entertainer.

5. THE ELASTIC STICKS

The magician uses two curved sticks—each more than a foot in length. One is painted black; the other is white. He compares the sticks and shows that the black one is larger than the white. He places them together, and presses on the ends until the condition is reversed—the white stick is larger than the black. Then he presses them until they both become the same size.

This trick is simply an adaption of an old optical illusion. The sticks are the same size—but one held below the other appears to be larger.

The clever part of the trick lies in the pretense of changing the sizes of the sticks. In placing them together, the white is set so that its end is further in than the black, but this is covered by the hands. By pushing forward on the white and drawing inward on the black, the condition appears to be reversed as is demonstrated by holding the black above the white. (The black was originally below the white.)

Again the sticks are brought together, the end of the black being further in, and they are apparently made the same size, as is shown by setting one on the other.

6. CHINESE WANDS

This is a method of restoring a cut string with the aid of a pair of Chinese wands, through which the string runs.

The wands are held side by side, and the string is drawn back and forth through them. Then the string is cut at the center; but is quickly restored, and drawn through the wands again.

Ever since the original "Pillars of Solomon" trick which is probably a hundred years old, magicians have sought to improve this idea so that the wands could be separated. With the "Chinese Wands," the string is actually cut; it is restored to its original length; it may be drawn from the wands and given for examination.

The wands are prepared thus:

Wand A has a projecting knob at the bottom. The wand is hollow, and the string passes through a hole in the top, down over the projecting knob, up in the wand again and out a hole on the other side. The wand is open at the bottom.

Wand B has a slit through which the string passes at the top, and the string also passes through a lead weight which is free inside the hollow wand. The wand is closed at the bottom. The slit at the top is not noticeable, as it is kept toward the performer and is camouflaged with painted lines.

The string is pulled back and forth through the wands. To all appearances it passes through holes in the upper ends of the wands and goes straight through. The magician creates this impression as he draws the string back and forth.

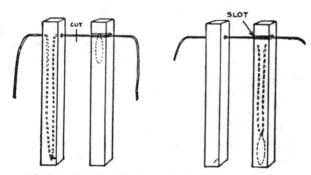

LEFT: The wands before the trick.
RIGHT: The wands after the trick.

He also calls attention to the exact length of the string. Then he invites some person to cut the string between the wands. This is done when the string is just about centered.

Now it will be observed that the string is actually much longer than it appears to be, due to the double length inside of Wand A. When the string has been cut, the magician brings the wands together and in so doing, he slips the string from the knob in the bottom of Wand A, releasing the extra length.

As he turns away, he seizes the center of the string, taking the cut end that protrudes from Wand A. He draws the string through the slit in Wand B, at the same instant raising the wands from the horizontal to the vertical. The sliding weight drops and carries with it the length of string that is projecting from either side of Wand B.

Thanks to the extra portion of string hidden in Wand A, the magician is now drawing a string back and forth—through the upper ends of the wands—and the string is quite as long as it was in the beginning!

The string may then be drawn clear of the wands and taken out for examination proving that it was restored. The wands, however, are laid aside.

7. MORE CHINESE WANDS

The effect previously described is ingenious; but it is of rather short duration. There is a newer trick which utilizes two wands with a restored string, and in this mystery the strings run while the wands are a foot apart.

The string is drawn back and forth between the wands; it is apparently cut; yet it runs just the same. And to prove that there is no connection the wands are set upright on a stand, and yet the string runs back and forth under the close scrutiny of the spectators.

The wands are a foot long and one inch square. There is a cord in each wand, and it runs down through to the bottom. These cords are connected by a black thread, two feet in length, which emerges from a hole in the bottom of each wand. Each string is just one foot long, and the free end has a tassel attached.

Half way up the side of one wand—on the outside—is a tiny hook. There is a depression in the other wand, so the two may be flush together. The thread runs over this hook and down to the bottom of the other wand.

At the outset, the string of one wand is pulled out to its full length. There is a foot of thread inside that wand; a foot of thread between the wands; and a string one foot long in the second wand.

By pulling on the short tassel, the string is apparently drawn through the wands at the tops—back and forth. This is done several times; then the string is apparently centered, and the wands are separated very slightly.

This reveals a dummy inch of string that is set between the wands at the top, to make it appear that the string actually runs through the top. The little length of string is cut.

The wands are then separated by raising the left wand (the one with the depression in the side). It can be carried six inches from the wand on the right.

When the wands are put together, the string can be drawn back and forth again. This is repeated several times.

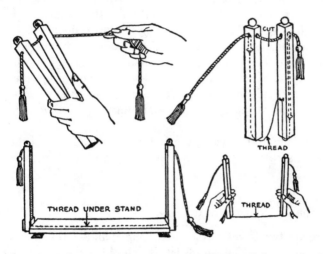

Now comes the perplexing part—the finish of the trick. The thread is slipped from the hook on the side of the right wand. The magician carries the wands to the stand, which is a flat pedestal one foot long, mounted on small feet.

A clamp is provided for each wand. The magician holds the wands upright, stretches them a full foot apart, and brings the lower end below the bottom of the stand. As he sets the wands in the clamps, which are at the extreme ends, the thread goes under the stand.

When he pulls the string on one wand, the other string shortens, and vice versa. The stand may be placed directly before the spectators, but they will detect nothing; for the thread is completely out of sight beneath the stand, where it runs under the bottom.

This final demonstration is the conclusion of the trick. The wands are left on the stand at the finish.

8 . THE CLINGING WAND

A magician's wand of the usual pattern is utilized in this effect. The wand rests on the table, and when the magician lifts the wand, it clings to his fingers in a mysterious fashion.

Either hand may be used—and the wand may be transferred from one to the other; yet it still retains its magnetic powers.

The wand has several pieces of thin black wire projecting from it, along one side. At a short distance these are invisible, especially as the wand is black; and the wand may be used for ordinary purposes.

In picking up the wand, the fingers are placed against the side, and are spread apart. From almost any position the wand will cling to the fingers.

9 . THE VANISHING WAND

There are two forms of the "Vanishing Wand"—excluding an old version which is now out of date. Each of these wands is demonstrated to be quite solid, but when the wand is rolled in a piece of paper, it disappears.

The first type of wand is made of glazed paper, but the tips are genuine metal. The end of the wand may be wrapped on the table. When the wand is rolled in paper, the tube thus formed is torn to pieces, leaving no trace of the wand. The ends are tossed carelessly aside with the other bits of paper, the greatest amount of tearing taking place near the center.

The second type is a much heavier wand that may be dropped on the floor. It consists of a series of jointed parts, which are held together by a length of heavy cord elastic. Over these are sections of metal tubing, painted black. These sections slide about a half inch along the wand. So they keep the jointed parts from collapsing.

Thus the wand is used as a regular wand. When it is to be vanished, it is wrapped in a sheet of paper; the end section is shifted, pushing the others along, and the wand is ready to collapse. The paper tube is crumpled with the wand inside.

10. DOUBLE PRODUCTION WAND

The purpose of this wand is to enable the magician to produce two silk handkerchiefs from his empty hands.

The wand is hollow, and the tip of one end is loose. Inside it is a loop of wire. A handkerchief is thrust into the loop, and is pushed into the wand. When the tip is replaced, the wand appears quite ordinary.

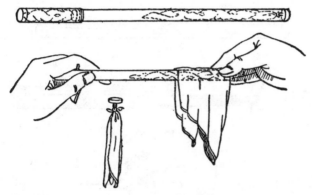

The first handkerchief is in the left end of the wand. The drawings show the removal of the second silk with the fake cap.

There is also an extra piece that fits on the other end of the wand—a piece of tubing less than three inches long which accommodates a twelve-inch silk handkerchief. This tube appears to be part of the wand.

The magician shows his hands empty and picks up the wand in his left hand, holding it by the extra piece. He puts the wand under his right arm, retaining the piece in his left hand. Bringing his hands together he produces the handkerchief.

In reaching for the wand, he attaches the extra piece of metal to the wand. He shows each hand empty, and lays the handkerchief over the other end of the wand. He seizes the center of the handkerchief with his right hand, holding the wand with his left; and as he draws the handkerchief away, he brings the tiny tip with it. He lays the wand on the table, and uses his right hand to draw the second silk from beneath the first. The little tip is laid on the table under the handkerchiefs.

11. FRANCISCUS HANDKERCHIEF WAND

In contrast to the clumsy and slow-working wands that have been devised to vanish a handkerchief, the wand invented by Franciscus stands out as a remarkable piece of apparatus.

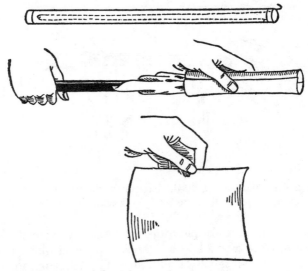

TOP: Construction of the fake wand.
CENTER AND BOTTOM: How the trick appears.

The effect of the trick is as follows: A piece of paper is rolled into a tube, and a handkerchief is pushed into the tube. To aid the progress of the silk, the magician picks up his wand and forces the handkerchief completely into the paper. Then he lays the wand aside. When the paper is unrolled, the silk has vanished.

The wand is hollow and is open at one end. A piece of cord elastic runs down into the wand, through a pulley at the solid bottom, and up the other side to the top where it is attached.

On the free end is a small nickel-plated tip, slightly smaller than the diameter of the wand. A groove underneath enables it to be fastened to the edge of the open end of the wand, where it holds the elastic taut. This metal tip has a hook soldered to it, the hook pointing downward.

When the handkerchief is in the paper, the magician pushes it further in with the wand. The hook catches the silk near the center. Then the end of the wand is tapped against the inner wall of the paper tube, and the tip is released. It is drawn rapidly to the bottom of the wand, taking the handkerchief with it.

12. THE HANDKERCHIEF PEDESTAL

The handkerchief pedestal is a well-known piece of magical apparatus, which is explained here because of its use in certain new combinations.

The pedestal stands nearly one foot high. A glass is placed upon it, and a cloth is thrown over the glass. When the cloth is removed a handkerchief (previously vanished) is seen in the glass.

The handkerchief comes from the pedestal. The glass is bottomless, and the handkerchief is pushed up by a mechanical action.

One type of pedestal has a spring to eject the handkerchief

which is just below the top of the pedestal. There are various models of this type.

The other type is operated by pressing down on the glass, thus lowering the top of the pedestal a little more than an inch, and forcing the handkerchief up with the rod of the pedestal. The change in height of the pedestal is not noticeable.

In both types the operation is quick and effective, and this piece of apparatus is usually very satisfactory.

13. HANDKERCHIEF AND GLASS PRODUCTION

The following trick utilizes the handkerchief pedestal. An empty tube is set on the pedestal. A handkerchief is vanished; and when the tube is lifted, the handkerchief is seen inside a glass on the pedestal. Both the glass and the handkerchief have appeared simultaneously.

The tube is of double thickness, with a space between the walls. The space is closed at the top of the tube, but not at the bottom. Hence the tube can be shown empty from one end, although a bottomless glass is concealed between its walls.

The bottomless glass in this case is virtually a cylinder of glass.

When the tube has been shown empty and placed upon the pedestal (which is of the spring type), the handkerchief is released, and it arrives in the tube. The tube is lifted leaving the glass with the handkerchief inside.

14. VANISHING GLASS AND HANDKERCHIEF

In connection with the preceding trick, the disappearance of a glass containing a handkerchief is an effective combination. A handkerchief is placed in a solid glass. Both are wrapped in a sheet of paper which is then crushed, showing that glass and handkerchief have vanished.

The glass has a celluloid lining. It is set on the table directly in front of a well or a servante. The handkerchief is inserted in the glass, and as the right hand takes the glass, the left hand holds the sheet of paper in front of it.

The right hand lets the glass slide into the well but retains the celluloid lining and the handkerchief.

These are shown and wrapped in the paper. The lining will pass as the glass at a very short distance. Then the paper is crumpled. Obviously the tumbler must have disappeared as it would be impossible to treat glass in such a manner.

The immediate reappearance of the glass and handkerchief heightens the effect.

Special celluloid linings can be obtained very cheaply as they are very thin and inexpensive to make.

15. EGG CLING CLANG

(With Handkerchief Pedestal)

This is a combination of several effects. An egg is set in a glass; the glass is placed on a pedestal and covered with a cloth.

A handkerchief is rolled in the hands, and becomes an egg. When the glass is uncovered, the handkerchief has taken the place of the egg.

Requirements: One handkerchief pedestal.

One hollow egg, with hole in the side.

Two silk handkerchiefs of the same color.

One bottomless glass.

The fake egg is dropped in the bottomless glass. The glass is covered with a cloth, and is lifted from the right hand, upon which it is resting.

The egg remains in the hand, which closes over it and palms it. When the glass is placed on the pedestal, the handkerchief in the pedestal is released.

The duplicate handkerchief is taken in the hands, and is worked into the hollow egg. Then the egg is shown and is laid on the table. The cloth is lifted from the glass to reveal the silk handkerchief.

16. MYSTERIOUS PENETRATION

The effect of this trick is unusual. A glass is filled with ink and is placed on the table. Two empty cylinders are exhibited, and one is placed over the glass.

A sheet of glass is set on the cylinder, and the other cylinder is placed on top. When the upper cylinder is lifted, the glass of ink is seen there, while the lower cylinder is empty.

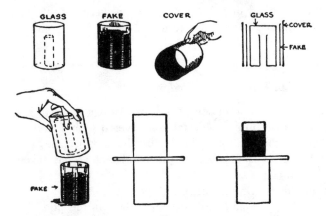

The glass used is of a special type, called the "Demon Glass." It is cylindrical, and it has a small cylinder in the center. The center portion being of glass also, it cannot be seen.

One of the two cylinders contains a tube of celluloid, painted black nearly to the top. The cylinders may be shown empty, as they are black inside, and the celluloid fake cannot be seen.

The cylinder containing the fake is placed over the glass—after the glass has been filled with ink. When the cylinder is lifted, the first two fingers enter the top and engage the center of the glass —one finger within; the other without. Thus the glass is lifted with the cylinder. But the celluloid fake remains, as it is larger than the glass, and everyone thinks it is the tumbler.

The other cylinder is placed over the celluloid fake. The sheet of glass is placed on the cylinder. The cylinder with the tumblerful of ink is immediately set upon the sheet of glass.

The upper cylinder is lifted showing the glass of ink. In showing the bottom cylinder, the celluloid fake is lifted with it and the tube may be shown quite empty.

17. THE CHINESE WONDER BLOCKS

Two black blocks, threaded on a piece of tape, with a tassel at the bottom to prevent them from falling. A bandana handkerchief is slipped over the tape, and a spectator is invited to hold the upper end of the tape.

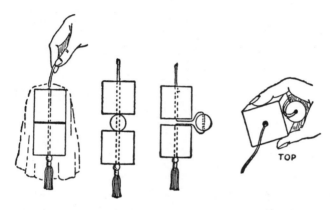

The magician shows a small gold ball. He puts it under the handkerchief, and immediately places it on the tape between the two blocks. Both the blocks and the ball have a hole in the center; and the entire apparatus is left in the hands of the audience, while they wonder how the ball managed to get between the blocks!

The ball is on the tape at the beginning. But it is pulled up behind the blocks. The blocks are three inches square; while the ball is only an inch and a half in diameter.

The left hand supports the blocks, holding them together, and keeping the ball hidden in the palm, while the right hand draws the ribbon back and forth through the blocks.

Then the handkerchief, which has a hole in the center, is slipped over the tape. The blocks are released, and the ball slides between them—the click being the natural noise of the blocks themselves.

The magician takes a duplicate ball and reaches beneath the handkerchief. He holds the ball palmed in his right hand, and lifts the handkerchief with that hand, showing the ball between the blocks.

As the spectators are not aware that a duplicate ball is used, this becomes a real problem.

18. COMEDY HAT LEVITATION

This is really a surprising trick; but it is also a good comedy effect.

The magician borrows a derby hat. He holds it in front of him, and suddenly removes his hands. The hat remains in the air. He passes his hands around the hat; walks forward and returns it to its owner, while everyone wonders what held the hat up.

Attach a thread to the center of a short black wand, and fasten the other end of the thread to a button of the vest.

Place the wand under the vest, with the lower tip under the belt.

Borrow the hat, and as you hold it in front of you, slide the wand down from under the vest, and swing the upper end forward. The tip of the wand presses against the body, and the belt acts as the fulcrum of a lever. The mouth of the hat should be toward you, and you merely hang the hat on the projecting end of the wand.

The hands may then be removed and passed around the hat, which seems to float in mid-air. To conclude the trick, push inward with the hat, and the wand will slide down the trousers leg; but the thread will stop it as soon as it is out of sight. The hat may then be returned to the owner and not a trace of the trick will remain.

19. THE BILLIARD BALL BOX
(*Improved by El Barto*)

This is the newest version of the "Billiard Ball Box" in which a billiard ball disappears from a box with two compartments. It is an improvement by El Barto, over his original box.

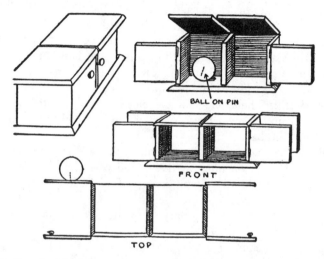

The box has four doors, and is divided into two compartments. Two of the doors are in front; two in back. The magician places the ball in one side of the box. Then he opens the doors and shows that the ball has gone. But it has been heard to slide to the other side. So he opens the doors there, after closing those of the first compartment. This process is repeated for some time. Finally all the doors are opened to show that the ball is not in the box.

The ball used is made of rubber—an imitation golf ball of the ten cent store variety is suitable. One back door of the box has a needle point projecting inward—and therein lies the secret.

The ball is put in that compartment; and when the doors are closed it is impaled on the needle. The box is tilted, and thanks to a sliding weight in the thin double bottom of the box, everyone thinks the ball has gone to the other side.

The first compartment is now shown. The back door is opened first, and the ball goes with it—out of sight in back of the box. Then the front door is opened.

While everyone is demanding that the other side of the box be shown, the performer makes away with the billiard ball, by one of two methods.

(A) He places his right hand in front of the opened back door and curls his fingers up underneath the door with the thumb coming down from above—as though about to close the door. Instead, he takes his hand away, and carries the ball with it, concealed in the palm of the hand. Then he closes the doors and opens the other side. While the spectators are shouting to "show the other side," believing that the ball has returned to the first compartment, the magician idly puts his right hand in his pocket and drops the ball.

(B) If the magician is using a table with a well, he sets the box on the table after opening the doors; and when he picks it up to show the other side, he simply knocks the ball loose and lets it fall in the well.

In complete form, preliminary steps are taken to arrange for the return of the ball.

The reproduction of the billiard ball is a little trick in itself. The magician uses a cardboard horn, of the New Year's variety. He shows this empty and drops the ball inside to prove it. He has a duplicate ball concealed in his hand, and when he turns the horn over, the first ball remains inside; but he places his hand beneath the horn and brings the palmed ball into view.

Then he sets the inverted horn on the table; lifts it, and sets it down again, this time with a slight thump which lets the ball drop to the table.

The ball in his hand is the one he vanishes from the box. The horn is then lifted to show the ball beneath.

20. PRODUCTION OF FOUR BOUQUETS

A cardboard flower pot is inverted upon a tray. It is lifted to show a bouquet of flowers. The flowers are removed; the trick is repeated, not once, but three times, four clusters of flowers being produced.

The flowers come from the tray. The center is divided into four sections, and each one operates on a spring. Thus there are four compartments, shallow, but large enough to contain fifty "spring flowers" each.

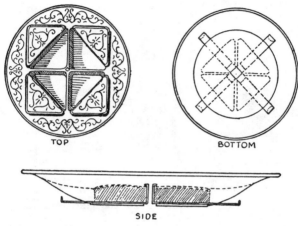

Upper left shows the containers open.
Upper right and lower drawings illustrate the releases.

The flowers of each bouquet are joined by light cords. The magician inverts the bowl on the tray—which is about twelve inches in diameter—and releases one section by a rod beneath the tray. The lid springs back automatically, releasing the flowers. The action is repeated with the other containers. The tray may be turned toward the audience at any time, for the pattern is designed to conceal the mechanism.

Each bouquet as withdrawn should be laid upon an ordinary tray. If an assistant holds the tray, and releases the flowers, a handkerchief can be used instead of the flower pot; the assistant making each release just as the tray is covered.

21. NOVEL PRODUCTION BOX

This is a box about ten inches long by five inches in width and five inches in depth—or similar proportions. The magician holds it toward his audience, and opens the top, which is a hinged lid. This reveals the interior of the box, and everyone can see that it is completely empty.

He closes the box and holds it in his left hand. Then he opens the lid and proceeds to extract many silk handkerchiefs and flags from the interior.

The box has two lids—one on top; the other on the bottom. Extending from side to side, and set diagonally across the interior of the box is a mirror—preferably of metal. The inside of the box is papered with fancy material.

The space behind the mirror is "loaded" with the handkerchiefs and flags. Both lids are closed, and the side containing the silks is set downward.

Picking up the box, the magician opens the lid, and reveals the interior. The mirror creates the illusion of an empty box. Upon closing the lid, the magician immediately shows all sides of the box to the audience; and this simple procedure enables him to turn it upside down. So when he opens the lid again, he has the compartment containing the handkerchiefs. He keeps the opening upward and produces the silks one by one.

If the audience is above the performer, he should set the box on the table, and open the lid part way—toward the spectators. This will conceal the interior of the box as he produces the handkerchiefs. By using a double-faced mirror, the handkerchiefs can be brought out in groups and the box be shown empty at the finish.

22. TWO NEW COIN STANDS

The "coin stand" is a little easel used by manipulators on which to rest coins. By a simple mechanical arrangement, the stand itself is used to effect the disappearance of several coins.

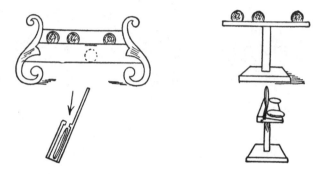

The first type of stand is a flat board set at an angle, with ornaments at the ends. The surface is covered with velvet, and a ledge runs along the center.

Four coins rest upon the ledge, setting in slight depressions. To the right of each coin is a slot, invisible in the velvet. If the coin is pushed to the slot, it will drop in and fall into the lower section of the easel; for the ledge is formed by an additional half-board superimposed on the front of the easel.

With four coins on display, the magician places his fingers upon the first one, and as he covers the coin, slides it to the slot. As the coin drops he pretends to take it in his hand, and to place it in the other hand—from which it disappears. The movement is repeated with the remaining coins. With virtually no skill, the magician can make coins vanish in a manner that rivals the best sleight of hand.

The second type of stand may be used for the production of

coins as well as for their disappearance. It is simply a flat bar, crosswise on an upright post. The coins stand on edge, in a ledge at the front of the bar. In covering a coin with his fingers, the magician lets it fall back on the bar, where it lies level, and cannot be seen because of the ledge.

With a single coin palmed in his right hand, the magician can have a row of coins out of sight on the stand. He lets the coin appear at his finger tips; apparently transfers it to the left hand, but retains it palmed in the right. The left hand, pretending it holds the coin, approaches the stand, and lifts up one of the coins. This is repeated with those that remain—every coin the right hand catches is placed upon the stand.

The inexperienced manipulator can use a mechanical coin for catching at the finger tips, if he chooses; but very little skill is required in using the stand.

23. NEW STYLE PRODUCTION BOX

A cubical box with no top or bottom is shown to be entirely empty. A rectangular tray is exhibited, and a piece of glass the size of the bottom of the box is placed upon the tray. Then the box is put on the glass.

Reaching in the box, the magician produces a quantity of silk handkerchiefs.

The handkerchiefs come from the tray. The tray is double, with a space between, and it has four tiny triangular traps near the center—these corresponding to the corners of the box when it is set on the tray.

When the glass is placed on the tray, it is turned so that it takes the position of a diamond instead of a square. When the box is placed upon it, the corners have access to the traps in the tray.

Several silks can be drawn from each trap, the ends of the silk being linked together so that one will draw the next from its hiding place.

The trick is specially effective when an assistant holds the tray.

24. THE BOGART TUBE

This is a stage trick which is suitable for platform performances, as it can be done with spectators on all sides. It is a trick that is not often seen, and one that has not been explained in any book on magic.

A nickel-plated tube, nine inches long, open at one end, is passed for examination. Then water is poured into it, and a piece of tissue paper is placed over the opening and is clamped there with a ring.

On the platform is a stand with a projection at the top; the projection holds a band about four inches in height, of larger diameter than the tube.

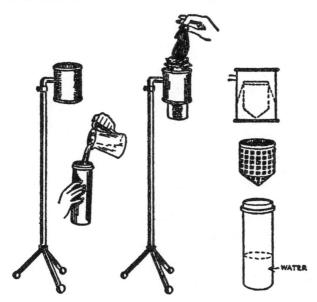

The magician inserts the tube in the band, and tilts the stand forward to show the unbroken tissue paper. Then he breaks the paper and produces an array of silk handkerchiefs ending with large flags. At the conclusion he removes the tube from the stand and pours out the water!

The "load" containing the handkerchiefs is in the metal band on the stand. It consists of an acorn-shaped metal tube, with holes in the sides; and a piece of tissue paper is over the opening, at the top, held there by a metal band.

The original tube is only half-filled with water. In inserting it in the band, it is pushed upward. The point of the acorn-loader pierces the tissue paper; but as the loader is slightly smaller than the tube, the tube picks it up, and the paper on the loader takes the place of the torn paper on the tube.

A flange on the tube catches in place and holds the tube in position in the band.

The magician breaks the paper and produces all the silks from the loader. Then he removes the tube—upward—and pours out the water which comes through the holes in the loader.

The loader is only about four inches deep; hence the water does not reach it before the production of the silks, as there is less than five inches of water in the tube.

The movement of putting the tube in position is natural and effective and the fact that the paper is not broken during the tube's passage through the band seems to preclude the possibility of anything having been secretly placed within the tube.

25. THE PASSING KNOTS

This is one of the most popular of handkerchief tricks—a clever effect that has been considerably improved since its invention some fifteen years ago.

The magician has two sets of handkerchiefs—three in each set. Red, white and blue were the original colors. Then all whites came into common use. The best combination is to have two reds and a blue in one set; two blues and a red in the other.

The magician picks up the two blues and a red; and places them in a tumbler or on a stand. Then he ties the blue between the two reds. Shaking these three handkerchiefs, the blue handkerchief falls free. Upon lifting the other set of silks, the red is seen to be tied between the two blues!

There are two phases to the trick: first the vanishing of the knots from the first set; second the appearance of the knots in the second set.

The first is accomplished by tying a trick knot. If an ordinary square knot is tied with the corners of two handkerchiefs, it will

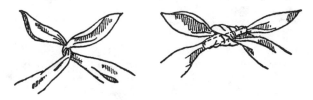

become a slip-knot if one corner is tied around the other. Tie the red around the blue; then pull the blue handkerchief straight, and it can be drawn free from the red.

But the quick vanishing knot is tied thus:

Simply cross the corners of the blue and red like a letter X. Bend the red under the blue and the blue over the red. Hold each handkerchief with the third and fourth fingers of the hands, while the thumbs and first two fingers tie a single knot with the corners.

This knot can be drawn very tightly; it will not pass the twist originally formed. Yet a mere shake of the handkerchiefs will cause the separation. In making the twist, the hands should be kept in motion, imitating the tying of a single knot.

The appearance of the knots in the other group of silks is simple: the knots are already there; but the side tips of the silks are tied, and not the upper and lower corners. The knots are concealed in the folds of the silks. The handkerchiefs are rolled together; when they are unrolled, grasp the side corner of one of the blue handkerchiefs, and shake them into a string of three.

This may be done without apparatus; but with the use of apparatus, the effect of the trick is increased. It is possible to show the handkerchiefs well apart before the trick begins.

The first method utilizes the table drape. Lay the three silks side by side on the table; then tuck the knotted corners down under the ribbon of the table drape. The silks will appear to be separate.

The second method is to drape the silks over a crossbar on an upright stand. The knotted corners are hidden behind the bar, and from in front the silks appear to be apart.

A special stand may be used; hollow at the back, into which the corners are introduced.

 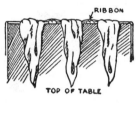

LEFT: The twist in the handkerchiefs.
RIGHT: The fake knot.

In picking up the silks from either of these positions, the magician must spread them out sufficiently to cover up the knots when the handkerchiefs are raised.

26. COIN ACT FINALE

A flashy trick is always effective at the end of a routine with coins. The old-fashioned "Coin Ladder" is an expensive apparatus that may be easily broken; and this newer variation, combining a table with the ladder effect is far more practical.

The magician sets a hat upon the table; places half a dozen coins in a glass; covers the glass with a handkerchief and sets it upon the hat.

As a center leg, the table has an upright plank with a molding; the plank is studded with nails and is fronted with a sheet of glass.

The magician taps the glass with his wand; the coins apparently pass through the hat, and appear one by one in the center leg, running down among the nails. They drop out the bottom into a bowl. Then the glass is shown empty.

Duplicate coins are used. The originals are dropped in a bottomless glass, ornamented at the lower edge. They fall into the performer's hand and he palms them away, dropping them in a pocket of his coat or the pocket of another table when he obtains the handkerchief.

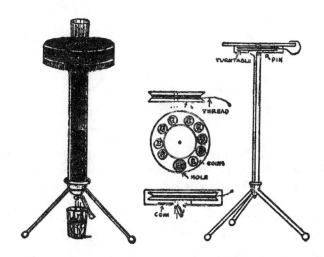

The duplicates come from beneath the table top. Two wooden discs are located there. The lower is firm and is grooved to hold the coins. It has a hole the size of a coin just above the opening of the upright plank. The upper disc revolves, being controlled by a cord passing out the back of the table. The magician draws this cord as he moves away. The upper disc revolves, and a nail in the disc pushes the coins so that they are forced into the frame, one by one.

CHAPTER THREE

The "Linking Rings" and the "Cups and Balls"

THE "Linking Rings" and the "Cups and Balls" are mysteries that will always be new, despite the fact that they have been performed regularly by magicians for the past century.

Their inclusion in this volume will be of great interest to all readers, experienced magicians as well as beginners, because the routines explained here represent the newest developments of these old favorites.

The routine of the "Linking Rings" is suitable for platform as well as stage, and involves a complete method of procedure which lacks complications, and which is performed with the usual set of eight rings. This is of special importance, as the eight ring set is standard and may be obtained from most magical supply houses.

The "Cups and Balls" were formerly dependent upon sleight of hand; but years ago a new method of presentation was evolved, and it has come into prominence because it eliminates all the difficult sleights and unnatural movements. With it, anyone may learn the trick; but the new method has never before appeared in a book on magic. With this volume as reference, the magician can learn the improved "Cups and Balls" and he will have one of the finest tricks of magic in his repertoire.

The descriptions of these tricks are easily understood when followed with the actual apparatus.

1. THE CHINESE LINKING RINGS

The "Linking Rings" mystery is more than a century old; but it still stands as the greatest trick in existence. The magical penetration of supposedly solid rings has all the semblance of real magic. Despite the fact that the trick has been exposed frequently, very few people can explain how it is done; and a clever magician can mystify people who know how the rings are constructed.

Psychologically the "Linking Rings" trick is perfect. A booklet could be written dealing with the reactions of those persons who witness its performance. Every magician has his own pet methods, so two performers rarely present the effect in the same way.

A mere knowledge of how the trick is done does not suffice. Therefore, comparatively few magicians are able to perform the trick. They know the secret of the trick, but they cannot present it.

Books on magic that explain the "Linking Rings" trick generally give a variety of moves; but when the beginner tries to perform them, he becomes confused and bewildered. He cannot work the different movements into an orderly procedure.

The whole secret of success is ROUTINE. The magician must practice a regular routine and learn it so that it becomes automatic.

Before describing the routine, we must first consider the construction of the rings. There are eight rings to the set, as follows:

Two single rings.

Two rings linked together.

Three rings linked together.

One "key" ring; a single ring which has an opening, large enough to admit the passage of another ring. The "key" ring is never closed. It does not lock; and it cannot be given for examination. When it is handled, the magician always keeps his fingers over the opening.

The rings are arranged in the following manner before presenting the trick.

The three linked rings are slipped on the right arm, up to the elbow. Then the "key" ring is placed on the arm; then the two linked rings; and finally the two single rings. The break in the "key" ring is hidden in the bend of the elbow.

The magician walks forward and states that he will pass all the rings for examination, and that as every ring is inspected, it will be placed on the left arm, so that the examined rings may be distinguished from those which have not been looked over.

He removes the two single rings with his left hand and gives one to a person on his left; the other to a person on his right.

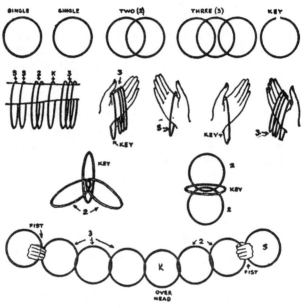

The illustrations show the entire set of linking rings; how they are placed on the left arm. The movements of exchanging the "key" for a single ring are shown also. Two designs—the "Stirrup" and the "Chain of Eight"—are also illustrated.

"Now," he states, "I will demonstrate what may be done with these rings. Watch!"

He takes the two linked rings with his left hand, holding them together, keeping the hand slightly in motion. No one knows that the rings are already joined.

"Here are two separate rings," says the performer.

He rubs the rings together, draws them apart and gives them a sudden twist. Then he holds them up—joined!

"Will you take these?" asks the magician, of a spectator. "Try to take them apart like I put them together. It's very easy—when you know how!"

This illusion is so deceptive, and so bold, that everyone believes the rings were originally separated. In print, this sounds strange. In practice, the ruse has been working for a hundred years.

The magician then takes the rings that are on his right arm, and holds them for a moment in his left hand, his fist covering the opening in the "key" ring. He turns to the man on his right who has the single ring, and takes the ring in his right hand.

Now comes an important and subtle move.

In turning to the person on his left, the magician drops the single ring along with the rings in his left hand. Then he throws the single ring and the three linked rings back on his right arm, retaining the "key" ring in his left hand.

The movement is so natural that everyone supposes the left hand is holding the single ring previously examined by the spectator on the right.

The "key" ring is transferred to the right hand. The left hand takes the single ring from the spectator on the left. The magician approaches the person who is holding the two linked rings.

"Again," says the magician, "I will show you how to put two single rings together. I will use these two single rings which *have just been examined and given back to me.*"

He rubs the "key" ring and the single ring together, with plenty of easy motion. This gives him an opportunity to slip the single ring through the opening in the "key" ring. The motion is kept up so that the spectators will not observe the exact moment of linking; then the rings are twisted and are shown joined, the single ring dangling from the "key."

"To take them apart," says the magician, "we reverse the procedure." He rubs the rings and slowly separates them. He lets the single ring fall on the left arm, and holds the "key" ring in the right hand.

"Give me your two rings," says the magician.

He takes them in the left hand and pushes the opening of the "key" ring through both sides of one of the two rings. Then he lets the two rings fall and holds the "key" ring. The two rings hang from the "key," and form a figure that resembles a stirrup.

The magician lifts one of the two rings and shows that the "key" ring is between them—but not connected. He slides the opening of the "key" through one side of the two rings, and lets the two rings fall. He then has a chain of three rings. His fingers cover the opening in the "key" ring.

Then he demonstrates how a ring may be removed by simply sliding the "key" ring off the upper ring of the two linked rings.

He lets the upper ring of the two linked rings slide on his left arm; then he puts the "key" ring on his left arm also, putting the opening of the "key" in the crook of his elbow.

Now comes the boldest part of the trick. Many performers slide through the following maneuver, and do not perform it effectively. On the contrary they should emphasize it, in the manner to be described.

"I will now," announces the magician, "present the most difficult feat ever attempted with the Chinese Rings. I will cause three separate rings to link together while in mid-air."

With his left hand, the performer seizes the three linked rings from his right arm. He holds them in his left fist, and with his right hand spreads them slightly apart at the outer extremity. He swings his left hand back and forth and suddenly tosses the rings in the air. As they fall, he catches one of the rings and exhibits the chain of three linked together, the rings dangling and clanging. The right hand grasps one end of the chain, the left hand the other. This bold procedure is extremely effective, and when the magician immediately gives the three rings for examination, the audience is greatly impressed.

The magician refers to his right arm and finds that a single ring remains there.

"Here," he says, "is one ring which has not yet been inspected. Will you please examine it?"

He gives the ring to a spectator. (The ring has, however, been examined before.)

Up to this point, the routine of the "Linking Rings" has been presented at close quarters. The magician asks for the return of the single ring, and places it on his *right* arm. He takes the chain of three in his right hand and moves a short distance from the audience. (In a hall, or theater, he goes to the center of the stage.)

The magician slides the "key" ring into his left hand, and transfers it to the right, holding the chain of three in his left.

"The climbing ring," he announces.

He starts the "key" ring at the bottom of the chain of three, slides it up the chain, and links it to the top ring. This movement must be practiced to make the link without hesitation. Performed gracefully, it appears as though the ring has moved up the chain link by link. At this point the magician may form fancy designs with the four rings. The formation of the designs will be explained later.

Taking the single ring from his right arm, and holding it in his right hand, the magician tosses it in the air once or twice, and then slides it up the chain, pushing its upper side through the opening in the "key" ring. He thus has a chain of five rings; but he must retain the "key" ring in his left hand, otherwise the opening would show.

In order to display the chain of five to good advantage, the magician should transfer the "key" ring to his right hand, and take the bottom ring of the chain in his left. Holding the chain horizontally in front of his body, he states that the rings now form a "Giant Watch Chain." The odd ring hanging from the "key" ring is the charm on the end of the chain, according to the magician.

The left hand immediately takes the "key" ring; the right hand seizes the odd single ring, and slipping it out of the "key" ring draws it down the chain and off the bottom. The optical illusion again takes place; the single ring appears to go from ring to ring in its passage down the chain. The single ring may then be given for examination, but this should not be prolonged, as the trick is now working to its climax.

The single ring is thrown on the right arm. The two linked rings are slipped off the left arm, and one of them is linked to the "key" ring, making a row of six.

While he is doing this, the magician states that he will form all eight rings in one long continuous chain. He slips the "key" ring over his head, so that the opening is behind his neck.*

Then he lets one single ring slide down each arm, catching one in each fist. The fists immediately grasp the end rings of the chain of six, and the arms are lifted, holding the row of rings in a horizontal position. The single rings are held so that they extend straight out; and they appear to be attached to the ends of the chain.

This is another bold part of the "Chinese Rings," and many magicians would hesitate to keep the long chain in position, fearing that suspicion would be attached to the end rings. On the contrary, the chain of eight is the formation most appreciated by the audience, and they become so bewildered by the previous actions of the rings that they never realize that the chain is not complete.

Bringing his hands together, the magician links the rings at random, mixing them on the "key" ring so that they form a jumbled mass.† He may conclude his performance at this point, bowing, and laying the rings aside; or, if he is on a platform or in a large room, he may finish by shaking the "key" ring violently, letting go of the opening. As a result, the rings will fall to the floor in groups, and the "key" ring may be tossed off in a corner where it will be out of sight.

Always make plenty of noise with the rings. The constant clanging is proof of their solidity, and it makes the trick more effective. The larger the rings the better.

There are dozens of possible variations with the "Linking Rings." Many of them are superfluous and weaken the effect of

---

* Some sets of rings are not large enough to pass over the head. In that event, the opening of the "key" ring should be taken between the teeth.
† *Never* arrange the rings so that they will hang on the "key" ring alone. The action calls attention to the one ring.

mystery. The preceding routine should not take more than five minutes, allowing for the examination of the rings. Performers who stretch the "Rings" to fill in fifteen minutes or more usually succeed in tiring their audiences.

Most of the variations of the "Linking Rings" are the formation of designs. A few of these are good. The best is the "Rocking Chair." The designs are formed immediately after the formation of the chain of four rings, with the "key" ring at the top.

To make the "Rocking Chair," twist the chain to the right, by means of the lowermost ring. Give the bottom ring a half-turn to the left, bring it up and immediately attach it to the "key" ring.

By bringing the "key" ring and the ring opposite together, a "Base-ball Mask," may be formed.

When the fist is held with the rings upward, and pressure is slightly released, the rings will spread out and form the "Opening of the Flower."

The position into which the rings then fall may be designated the "Square of Circles."

When the rings are shaken, they will form a three link chain, the center of which is double. When the bottom ring is brought up along with the "key" ring, the performer has a "Giant Chain," formed with two double links.

At the conclusion of the designs, one ring must be loosened from the "key" ring in order to come back to the chain of four.

THE DROPPING RING

(*An Additional Move*)

This is a very unusual movement with the "Linking Rings," used when there are four together (three rings and "key").

In effect, a ring goes link by link from the top of the chain to the bottom.

The Method: Hold the "key" ring at the top and twist the bottom ring to the right, forcing all the rings as far as they will go in that direction.

Then swing the bottom of the chain upward, so the "key" ring becomes the lowest of the chain.

Slide the "key" ring toward you. Then bend it back, until it is nearly flat against the ring to which it is connected—just like closing a book. Raise the right hand again, still holding the other end of the chain with the left hand.

You will now have two rings supported by the right hand—the "key" ring in the fist, and the top ring of the chain of three, which rests on the knuckles of the right hand.

Shake the ring from the knuckles, and it will drop to the ring below. Let it stay there an instant; then slightly release pressure with the left hand; and the middle ring of the chain of three will drop to the bottom ring. Now let go of the bottom ring, and it will fall with a clang on the bottom of the chain.

The illusion created is that one ring has dropped link by link from top to bottom. In reality, another ring has taken up the journey at each step.

ADDING THE "KEY" RING

An effective way of presenting the Ring trick is to pass all the rings for inspection at the beginning. First, two singles; then link two and pass them out; then link three and pass them for examination.

When this is done, the "key" must be secretly added to the other rings.

Method One: Place the "key" ring under the coat, hanging it over a fountain-pen in the vest pocket. Button the coat. Gather the examined rings in the left hand. Hold the hand at the bottom of the coat.

In turning to the left to receive an odd single ring, press against the left side of the coat with the right hand, thus raising the hidden "key" ring. As the right hand reaches toward a spectator, the "key" drops from beneath the coat, and is caught by the fingers of the left hand, so that it joins the other rings.

Method Two: Lay the "key" ring on a chair. Cover it with a handkerchief and lay the other rings on top of it. Proceed with the solid rings, and as you receive them, lay them on the chair. Pull the handkerchief up through the rings and toss it aside or put it in your pocket. This leaves the "key" at the bottom of the pile, and it is picked up with the others.

Method Three: This is with pocket sized rings—between three and four inches in diameter. Slip the "key" over the wrist and up the sleeve. Proceed with the solid rings, and as they are returned, slip them on the wrist. In removing them, the thumb goes up the sleeve and brings the "key" ring along with them.

2. THE CUPS AND BALLS

The following routine with the "Cups and Balls" serves to modernize the famous old trick; and possesses the great advantage of requiring no sleight of hand. All that is necessary is to acquire a thorough knowledge of the routine, which may then be worked at a fairly rapid speed; not too quickly to be confusing; but rapidly enough to leave the keenest spectator far behind.

The outfit consists of three nickel-plated cups, which are identical in appearance. In practicing the movements, it is wise to paste a small label to each cup, marking the cups A, B, and C. These letters are used in the directions. In actual working, of course, the labels should be removed. Besides the cups, seven small balls of sponge rubber are used. These are preferable to the old-style cork balls, as they do not "talk."

The trick should be performed on a box about twelve inches long, seven inches wide, and six inches deep. Behind the box are three pieces of tubing, about one inch in length. Each piece of tubing is set upright; and on each tube is set a rubber ball, orange (tangerine), potato, or any other spherical object which may be wedged up into one of the cups.

Preparation. Before showing the trick, drop a rubber ball in cup A, and then insert cup B, in cup A. Drop a ball in cup B, and insert cup C (of course these are the small balls of sponge rubber). The cups will nest perfectly, because their peculiar construction leaves a space between their bottoms.

Place the five remaining balls to the left of the box.

The "Key" Move. The success of the trick depends upon a "key" move, which is quickly learned. Hold the cups in the left hand, with the mouths up. Now with the right hand, remove the bottom cup, and with a swing of the forearm turn the cup mouth down and bring it smartly down on to the box. The ball will not fall from the cup during this operation; it will be trapped beneath

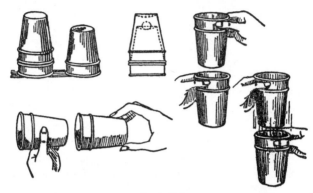

At the left the concealment of a ball between cups is shown; also the method of setting a cup on the table. At the right the illusion of dropping one cup through another is given in detail.

the cup. The movement is so clean and natural that no one will suspect there is anything beneath the cup. Whenever a cup is set mouth down on the table, it is always with this movement, whether the cup is empty or not.

Setting Down Cups. The three cups, nested, are set on the table, mouth down, and in the following directions, whenever the text reads "set a cup on the table" or "set a cup on another cup," the directions mean to set the cup down, *unless otherwise stated.*

Move One. The various operations are called "moves." The cups are set mouth down, nested, in the order (top to bottom) A, B, C.

Remove cup A and set it at the right of the box. Remove cup B and set it at the left. Place cup C in the center.

Move Two. Place one of the five visible balls on cup A. Set cup C down on cup A, rather forcibly, as though to drive the ball through. Pick up the two cups together and reveal a ball beneath cup A.

Move Three. Remove cup C from cup A and set it on cup B. (There is a ball in cup C which will be trapped between the cups C and B.) Pick up the ball which appeared beneath cup A, set it on cup C and set cup A on top of cups C and B.

Move Four. Lift all three cups together, and show that the ball has "passed through."

Now remove cup A, placing it at the right; remove cup C setting it down on the ball at the left, and place cup B in the center.

Continue by taking the second of the five visible balls. Place it on cup A at the right. Set cup B on top, and lift both cups showing the ball beneath.

Move Five. Set cup B on cup C. Put the ball on cup B. Place cup A on cup B and lift all three cups, showing *two* balls beneath.

Move Six. Set cup A at the right; cup B on the two balls at the left, and cup C in the center. Pick up the third original ball; place it on cup A. Set cup C on cup A. Lift both cups, showing the ball beneath.

Move Seven. Put cup C on cup B. Put the ball on cup C. Set cup A on cup C. Lift all three cups and show *three* balls beneath.

Move Eight. Set cup A at the right; cup C on the three balls at the left, and cup B in the center. Pick up the fourth original ball. Place it on cup A. Set cup B on cup A. Lift both cups showing the ball beneath.

Move Nine. Set cup B on cup C. Put the ball on cup B. Put cup A on cup B. Lift all the cups and show four balls beneath.

Move Ten. Set cup A at the right; cup B on the four balls at the left; cup C in the center. Put the fifth visible ball on cup A. Set cup C on cup A; lift both cups and show the ball beneath.

Move Eleven. Place cup C on cup B. Put the ball on cup C; set cup A on cup C. Lift all three cups and show five balls beneath.

Note: Up to this point it will be noticed that each pair of moves repeats the previous pair, with one more ball appearing at the left each time.

Move Twelve. Set cup A at the right; cup C on the five balls;

cup B in the center. Catch an imaginary ball from the air; toss it at cup A. Lift cup A and show the ball.

Move Thirteen. Set cup B aside. Put the ball on cup C. Set cup A on cup C. Lift the two cups together and reveal six balls. Immediately take cup A from cup C and set it on cup B. Exhibit cup C and then lay it aside.

Move Fourteen. Pick up cups A and B. Remove cup A and set it on the box. Take one of the balls, set it on cup A; put cup B on cup A. Lift both cups and show the ball beneath.

Move Fifteen. Set cup B on the ball; put a ball on cup B; put cup A on cup B. Lift both cups and show the *two* balls beneath.

Moves 16, 17, 18 and *19.* Move 16 is a repetition of 14; putting cup A on the two balls; but this time three balls are beneath the cup. Move 17 repeats 15, with four balls appearing beneath. Moves 18 and 19 are likewise repetitions of the preceding moves, producing five and six balls, respectively. At the end of move 19, lift both cups; remove cup A (which will be on cup B), and set cup A on cup C. Then show cup B with the six balls.

*   *   *   *

Penetrating Cups. At this point it is a good plan to introduce the effect of dropping one cup through another. Pick up cups A and C, and remove cup A; turn it bottom down, and let the ball contained in the cup slide into your right hand. Pass cup C for inspection, and do likewise with cup A, dropping the extra ball behind the box.

Take back the cups, and hold one, *mouth up,* between your left thumb and second finger. Drop the other cup (*mouth up*) into the cup in your left hand, and let it knock the cup out of your hand—your thumb and fingers catching the cup just dropped from the right hand. The effect is that you dropped one cup right through the other. This may be repeated and given as a pseudo explanation of why the balls went through the cups.

*   *   *   *

The Big Finish. Set three of the small rubber balls on the box, and lay a cup in back of each ball, the mouths of the cups toward the spectators. Pick up the right cup with the right hand; show it casually, pick up the ball with the left hand; as you exhibit the ball, set the cup, mouth down behind the table, on the big ball at the right. Press the cup over the ball and it will pick it up. Then put the cup mouth down on the table and set the small rubber ball on top of it.

Repeat with the other two cups.

Lift the right cup, showing nothing beneath it (the big ball being wedged). Set the cup down with a bump, and the big ball will drop and rest loose beneath the cup. Perform the "French Drop" vanishing the small rubber ball; lift the cup and reveal the big ball. Get rid of the small ball behind the box.

Repeat this procedure with the two remaining cups.

*   *   *   *

Notes

Cups Upon Balls. If you experience trouble setting a cup over all the balls in moves 11 and 19, group four balls together and set the fifth on top, making a pyramid. As you set the cup down on the balls, if any start to escape, you can lift the cup slightly, and draw them in with the edge.

The Whirligig. When you take a cup containing a concealed ball, hold the cup mouth up in your right hand, and you can toss it in the air, letting it describe a complete revolution. Toss the cup easily, and catch it upright. Then set the cup down as previously described. This move should only be used occasionally, and it should be done several times with cups that are *actually empty,* allowing a glimpse of the interiors as you set down the empty cups.

The French Drop. This consists of holding a ball between the thumb and forefinger of the left hand. Right hand fingers encircle ball and apparently remove it; but ball is secretly allowed to drop in left hand.

New Additional Routine

The following moves may be introduced when the production of large balls is impractical, as is sometimes the case. The additional routine may also be used in connection with the regular movements.

Refer back to the Note following "move eleven." At this point, the three cups have been lifted showing five balls beneath. From bottom up the cups are B, C, and A. There is a ball beneath cup C and a ball beneath cup A.

Eliminate "moves 12 and 13." In their place do as follows: Set cup A at the right. Set cup C at the left. Pick up one of the five balls that are on the table and set it on cup A. Then execute move 14, and follow with 15, 16, 17, and 18. You will then have cup B on cup A; and when the two cups are lifted, five balls will be seen beneath.

Move Twenty. Set cup B on cup C. Pick up a ball and set it on cup B. Drive cup A down upon cup B. Lift all three cups showing ball beneath.

Move Twenty-one. Set cup A over the single ball. Set cup B on cup A. Put a ball on cup B and drive down cup C. Lift all three cups showing two balls beneath.

Move Twenty-two. Cup C on the two balls; cup B on C. Put a ball on cup B and drive it through with cup A. Lift cups showing three balls beneath.

Move Twenty-three. Cup A on three balls; B on A; ball on B; drive cup C down on B; lift three cups showing four balls.

Move Twenty-four. Cup C on four balls; cup B on C; ball on B; set A on B and lift all three cups showing five balls.

Final Moves. Set cup A on the table (a ball going beneath it). Set cup B on cup A (a ball being under cup B). Set cup C on cup B. Then lift cup C in a very matter-of-fact manner. There is no ball beneath cup C. Tap cup C with the hand or wand, calling attention to its solidity, and set it mouth up on the table, with the right hand.

The left hand slides the cups B and A over by the five balls that are lying on the table. The right hand picks up the two cups together, and at the same instant, the left hand sweeps up the five balls, taking with them the ball which was beneath cup B, and which was left on the table when the two cups were lifted. The balls are deposited in cup C.

Cups B and A are lifted together. Cup A is set on the table (a ball going beneath it). Cup B is then placed on cup A (no ball beneath).

Cup B is casually lifted and shown empty. It is tapped to show its solidity. The balls are poured from cup C into cup B and from cup B into the left hand, cups B and C being set mouths upward. The left hand, filled with balls, slides along the table to cup A, which is tilted upward as on a hinge, while the left hand shoves all the balls into cup A, along with the ball which is already there. Cup A is then set aside, mouth upward.

The magician picks up cups B and C and states that although they are solid, it is really possible to drive a solid object through them, as he has previously demonstrated with the balls. He then goes through the business of apparently dropping one cup through another (see "Penetrating Cups") and gives the two cups for immediate examination. The spectators are thoroughly mystified, and the magician thus concludes his exhibition of the "Cups and Balls," laying them all aside.

Note: A good way of secretly obtaining a ball from beneath a cup is the following: Slide the cup forward along the table, tilting it forward slightly so that the ball is pressed under the edge of the cup. Then press the cup flat on the table, and continue to push it forward. The ball will pop out the back and will come into the palm of the hand which should be flat on the table.

By drawing the cup toward oneself, and tilting it slightly forward, a ball may be introduced beneath the cup, by a reversal of the procedure just described.

These movements require skill, and they are not essential to the routine of the "Cups and Balls." They are worth practicing, however, as they sometimes help the performer out of an emergency.

Conclusion: The additional routine is a good one, because it eliminates the pretended catching of a ball from the air. Seven balls are used throughout the trick; but the spectators believe that only five are employed.

The person who practices the "Cups and Balls" will probably introduce various movements of his own origination, as the possibilities are limitless.

When the performer has mastered the routine—which depends upon memory, and not upon skill, he will soon forget all about cups A, B, and C. He will find that each move leads logically to the next, and no great memory work will be required. A smooth, finished routine should be performed leisurely, but without hesitation, with constant patter, to keep the spectators' attention on each penetration. The result will be a finished exhibition that is thoroughly bewildering and mystifying.

CHAPTER FOUR

Mental Mysteries and Spirit Tricks

UNDER this heading comes various forms of mystery that are akin to magic. The important distinction between these secrets and those of the usual type of magic lies in their method of presentation and the effect that the performer seeks to create.

They can be shown as tricks, pure and simple, if desired; but where a trick is naturally attributed to skill or mechanical deception, mental mysteries are usually considered (by the spectators) to be a form of concentration or even of telepathy; while many people are prone to attribute spirit tricks to some psychic force.

In showing mental mysteries, the performer should take advantage of the attitude of his spectators. It is quite permissible to make simple tricks virtually unexplainable by assuming an air of mystery and talking vaguely about psychology and mental concentration. But with spirit tricks, the various effects should be presented as duplications of so-called psychic phenomena, accomplished by natural means.

There are certain mind-reading stunts that can be classified either as mental mysteries or spirit tricks. It is rather difficult to draw a distinctive line between these two types of magic; hence they are grouped together, in this book.

Without question, this type of entertaining has come into great popularity today; it is a form of magic that is of comparatively recent development, although many of the basic principles have been used for many years. Many magicians are now specializing in mental and psychic effects, and the up-to-date performer should certainly include tricks of this nature in his repertoire.

MENTAL MYSTERIES

The methods described in this section are designed primarily for the use of one person, eliminating the codes and similar methods of transmission used in the two-person mind-reading acts.

1. NAMING THE NUMBER

The performer gives a pad and pencil to a person and requests him to write any number of three different figures. Then he is to reverse that number and write the smaller above the larger. Example: 382, reversed, 283.

When this has been done, the performer tells him to draw a line under the numbers and to subtract the smaller from the larger. After he has made the subtraction, the magician concentrates and then names the result.

First we must note a peculiarity that is evident in any subtraction of this type:

The answer will always be one of these numbers: 99, 198, 297, 396, 495, 594, 693, 792, 891. Of these numbers, 198 and 891 are very uncommon.

The performer pays little attention to his subject until the man is making the subtraction. Then the magician watches him from a distance, and notes his hand or the tip of his pencil.

If only two figures are written, the answer is 99. If three figures are written, the performer has only to identify one (except the center figure which is always 9).

This is an extremely easy matter which can be done on the first trial; and after some experience the performer can catch one of the numbers by a mere glance at the proper moment. Yet he is too far away to see the writing on the paper, or he cannot see it because of the elevation of the pad so no one will suspect anything.

Remember that the subtraction is from right to left. The center number is always sure. There is a distinct difference in the movement of the hand when it makes a 2 or a 6, and one figure caught gives the clue to the whole number.

2. GIANT MEMORY

To perform this mystery, the magician must have a card prepared exactly as shown below.

77	5	70	24	97	91	13	64	89
684268	415617	976392	336954	601123	001123	224606	576774	897639
11	12	90	94	48	60	9	41	99
022460	123583	998752	301123	752796	965167	819099	055055	801123
39	42	4	16	84	37	86	2	68
842684	156178	314594	527965	392134	640448	594370	112358	774156
3	87	21	75	56	49	10	23	32
213471	695493	033695	482022	561785	853819	910112	235831	145943
40	30	59	38	29	72	55	57	15
943707	932872	864044	741561	831459	189763	460662	662808	426842
51	79	66	65	85	26	92	88	71
066280	886404	572910	471897	493257	538190	101123	796576	088640
22	74	46	34	83	81	47	52	19
134718	581909	530550	347189	291011	099875	651673	167303	812224
69	14	93	25	45	6	33	35	67
875279	325729	201123	437077	459437	576730	246066	448202	673033
50	31	82	73	36	54	95	1	98
954932	044820	190998	280886	549325	369549	401123	011235	701123
80	62	8	58	18	76	28	78	7
987527	178538	718976	763921	729101	583145	730336	785381	617863
44	27	53	63	96	61	17	43	20
358314	639213	268426	279651	501123	077415	628088	257291	921347

Chart used in the "Giant Memory" trick.

He gives the card to a spectator and tells him that he has memorized 99 numbers of six figures each—nearly six hundred different figures, and that he has identified each one with a number between 1 and 100.

For example, if the spectator will ask "Name number sixty," the magician will immediately respond with 965,167. This terrific range of knowledge covers numbers from 1 to 1,000,000!

The test starts. Every number that is called meets with an instant response—and a correct one—from the magician. There is a key to the trick that makes it a simple matter of mental mathematics.

Add 9 to the number the spectator calls, and reverse the total for your first two figures. Example: Number 60. Add 9, making 69; reverse, and give 9–6 as your first two figures.

For the third figure, add the first two and give the total. If it is more than 10, drop the figure 1.

Example on 60: 9 and 6 (first two figures) total 15. Drop the 1, and name 5.

The fourth figure is obtained by adding the second and third in precisely the same manner. Example on 60: Add 6 and 5 making 11. Drop the 1 and name 1.

Similarly the fifth figure is obtained by adding the third and fourth. Example of 60: 5 and 1 total 6.

The sixth figure is obtained by adding the fourth and fifth. Example on 60: 1 and 6 total 7.

To make the task easier, use a blackboard. Write the numbers in order so all can see them. Here you have the numbers before you, and you can easily add them according to the simple rule.

3. BOARDS AND CARDS

This is an improvement over an older trick with cards; in this form it is very effective.

The magician gives out six envelopes each containing six different cards. He asks the persons who receive the envelopes to remember one card each, replacing all the cards in the envelope.

Then the magician holds up a board with six cards attached. He asks each person if he sees his card on the board. If the person says "Yes," the magician immediately names the card, even though he does not see the face of the board.

This is repeated with the remaining boards until the cards have been named. Sometimes two or more persons will have a card on one board—sometimes none.

Each board has one card from each envelope. The envelopes are numbered from 1 to 6. Now these duplicate cards are not definitely arranged on the board—they are there at random, but on the back of the board the magician has a tiny list.

For example: 1—JS: 2—10H: 3—AS: 4—9C: 5—4H: 6—QC.

These abbreviations stand for jack of spades; ten of hearts; ace of spades; nine of clubs; four of hearts; queen of clubs.

Each board is similarly arranged.

The magician picks up any board, and without looking at the front of it, holds the cards toward the spectators.

If the man with envelope 1 says he sees the card he mentally selected, the magician simply notes number 1 on the list and names that card. He does the same with any board and any number.

4. THOUGHT FORETOLD

The magician requests that some person mentally select the name of a playing card. Then the magician writes something on a slip of paper and throws it into a hat.

He puts the hat to one side and gives the spectator a pack of cards. He asks him to look through the pack—face up—and to drop his card on the table so that all can see it.

This is done. The magician picks up the hat, carries it to the spectator and lets him lift out the piece of paper. On it is written the name of the mentally selected card!

The magician has two pieces of flat wood or fiber. There are twenty holes drilled in the narrow edges of each—ten holes to a side; and four in each end.

The magician has tiny slips of paper bearing the name of every card in the pack. One piece of wood is used for black cards. The paper pellets are rolled and inserted in the holes with the king, queen and jack of spades at one end, and ace to ten at the side.

The other end has king, queen and jack of clubs; with ace to ten of clubs on the other side.

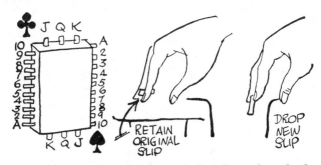

Illustrating one of the index boards used in the pocket; also how the substitution of slips is made.

The other board is similarly arrayed with hearts and diamonds. The black board goes in the left trousers pocket; the red board in the right.

Now for a bit of easy sleight of hand.

The magician writes anything on a slip of paper—and pretends to throw it in the hat, but retains it between his fingers. While the pack is being spread out he drops the slip in his coat pocket.

The instant the chosen card is revealed the magician puts his left hand in his pocket, if it is black; and his right hand in his pocket if it is red. The index board enables his fingers to obtain the slip that bears the name of the chosen card.

Let us suppose it is the ten of clubs.

In about one second the performer has the slip between the fingers of his left hand. With his right hand he picks up the hat by the brim. As he walks boldly toward the spectator, he grasps the hat at the side with his left hand; thumb beneath the brim and fingers just inside the hat. He instantly releases the slip of paper. It falls naturally in the hat. The spectator sees it there— the very piece (he thinks) that was thrown in at the beginning. He removes it and finds the name of his card!

5. THE MAGIC SQUARE TEST

The magician marks out twenty-five squares on a large sheet of paper or a blackboard. He states that he will fill those squares with numbers that will total the same in every direction on every line of five rows, vertical, horizontal, or diagonal.

This sounds difficult enough, but he adds that he will make that total equal any number desired, from sixty up to five hundred.

A number is given—one hundred and twelve, for example—and he fills the squares with numbers that bring the desired total in every direction.

The first secret is the method of forming a magic square. This is shown in the diagrams. You imagine that your square of 25 blocks is the center of nine similar squares.

LEFT: A magic square adding 65 in all directions.
RIGHT: How the square is formed.

Put the number 1 in the middle block of the top cross row. Then proceed one square upward to the right—in a diagonal direction, to place the number 2.

As this takes you out of your square, you must transcribe the number in the corresponding block of your square—namely, in the second from the right on the bottom row.

Continue thus—always one step up to the right, transcribing when you go over the edge.

Whenever your diagonal path is blocked by the presence of a number, drop straight downward one square and put in the number; then continue your diagonal journey.

This is done with numbers from 1 to 25. The result will be a magic square that totals 65 in every direction.

Now note five key squares thus:

```
X    *    *    *    *
*    *    X    *    *
*    *    *    *    X
*    X    *    *    *
*    *    *    X    *
```

These are indicated by the letter X. The simple addition of 1 to each of those squares will raise your total from 65 to 66.

Instead of the numbers 17, 7, 22, 12, and 2, those blocks must bear the numbers 18, 8, 23, 13, and 3—which duplicate other numbers on the board.

Add 2 to each of these squares to make a total of 67 in every direction; add 3 to make 68, and 4 to make 69.

Similarly by subtracting 1, 2, 3, or 4 from the key squares you can produce 64, 63, 62, or 61.

The important number to remember is 60, which is the key to the whole system. First subtract 60 from the desired number and divide by 5. That tells you the number to put in the first block.

Suppose 65 is chosen. Subtract 60, leaving 5; divide by 5 and you obtain 1, so you start your progression with 1—a fact which you already understand.

Suppose 70 is given. You subtract 60 and divide by 5—the result is 2, so you start your progression with 2 and end with 26.

If 365 is given, subtract 60, leaving 305. Divide by 5, obtaining 61. Start your numbers with 61, follow with 62, 63, and so on.

Thus it is a very simple bit of calculation to obtain a square of any number that is divisible by 5.

But suppose you get a number like 248. That offers no difficulty. You merely employ the rule given before. 60 from 248 is 188. Divide by 5 and you have 37 as your starting number. But you must take care of your remainder of 3. This is done by the simple process of adding 3 to each of the key squares as you proceed with the progression.

It is important to note that the key squares have no bearing on the others. You merely add 3 to the number which should ordinarily go there, and continue the progression as though you had not made the addition.

With a number like 299, it is better to work from 300. Subtract 60, leaving 240; divide by 5, giving 48 and use that as your number for the original block. But when you come to the key squares, subtract 1 in each instance.

These key numbers will duplicate other numbers on the board, but there are only five of them, and they are quite permissible.

The making of a magic square in itself is mystifying to the average person as few know the rule. But with this tremendous addition of making the lines total any desired number, the effect becomes immense. The rules cannot be learned without a little study, but they are well worth the effort. The performer who does this trick will be credited with amazing mathematical or mental ability. Plenty of time can be taken in calculation.

6. FIVE CARDS AND FIVE PELLETS

Five cards chosen by five spectators; and each person receives a slip of paper upon which he writes the name of this card. He rolls the slip into a ball and lays it upon the card, which is face down.

The magician tosses the paper balls into a glass, and picks up the five cards. Then he orders the balls to be rolled on the table. At his instruction, four of the persons each pick up a paper ball.

The magician drops one of the cards on the table, and puts the remaining paper ball upon it. When the ball is unrolled, it is read, and we will presume it says "Eight of Clubs." The card is turned up—and it is the eight of clubs!

Of course it can be done when all the cards are alike—that's not a bad idea—but in this trick a borrowed pack is used. The secret lies in the paper balls.

First of all, the slips are roughly torn and they vary in size. As no two people will roll a paper ball alike, the result is five different balls, varying slightly in size.

In picking up the cards upon which the balls rest, the magician takes the one with the smallest ball first—and so on—following in order of size—or noting any other slight difference in the pellets.

When the balls are rolled from the glass, four of them are picked up, one by one. The magician easily detects which remains —number one, two, three, four or five; and he tosses the corresponding card on the table.

7. DOUBLE PREDICTION

This is a combination of several methods, used in an unusual mental trick involving a pack of cards, some blank cards and an envelope. The magician writes the name of a playing card, with a colored pencil, on a blank card, and seals the writing in the envelope; he later writes the name of another card on a blank card in black and puts it in his pocket. Both of these cards prove to be cards that spectators choose from the pack at random.

Inside the envelope, the performer has a piece of colored carbon paper, pasted to the face of the envelope. This may be green, red, or any other distinctive color in which carbon paper may be obtained.

In his right trousers pocket, the performer has a card and a very short black lead pencil.

He begins by writing the name of any card in red, on one of several blank cards that are in his left hand. He gives a quick flash of the writing, so that all may see it, without reading it. Holding the cards in his left hand, he apparently draws away the card with the writing, but draws a blank card instead, marks it with the spectator's initials, and puts it in the envelope, which is sealed. This exchange is quite simple, as no one expects it.

All the cards are pocketed except one. The performer holds the envelope in his left hand, and a blank card upon the envelope. He asks a spectator to pick a playing card from the pack, and to turn it face up on the table. We will suppose it is the four of hearts.

"A red card," remarks the performer. He points to another spectator. "You *think* of a certain playing card—but make it a *black* one."

The performer draws a black pencil from his pocket.

"I used a colored pencil before," he says, "now I shall use a black one. Keep thinking of your card—I shall try to get your thought."

So saying, he writes something on the blank card that rests upon the envelope. The spectators naturally suppose that he is trying to catch the person's thought, and is writing the name of a black card. Instead, he is writing "Four of Hearts"—the name of the card first selected, and that is being transcribed in color on the card within the envelope!

Having finished his writing, the performer lays the envelope on the table, and puts the card with the black writing in his pocket. In so doing, he folds it, and pushes it up into the corner of the pocket.

"Name the card you chose," he says to the second spectator.

"Jack of clubs," replies the chooser.

"That's right!" exclaims the performer. "But just to verify it will you first remove the jack of clubs from the pack?"

Putting his hand in his pocket, the moment that attention is on the pack, the performer takes the tiny pencil and writes "Jack of Clubs" quickly on the blank card that is there. He immediately pushes the pencil up into the corner of the pocket, and brings out the card, at the same time turning the pocket inside out to show it apparently empty. He hands the card to the spectator—the name of the chosen card is upon it.

Then the envelope is opened, and the name of the card first selected is found on the card within, the envelope being torn and pocketed.

8. IMPROVED BOOK TEST

One of the most convincing of mental tricks is the divination of a word chosen at random from a book. The performer may ask a spectator to think of the chosen word; whereupon the performer names it; or the word may be discovered upon a spirit slate.

Now there are several ways of doing this, which I shall enumerate briefly before explaining the new system.

(A) Every page in the book is the same; that is, a prepared book is used.

(B) A certain word is at the same position on every page—such as the seventeenth word. The number seventeen must be "forced"; any page may then be used. This also requires a special book.

(C) A card is inserted at the proper page from the top of the book; the performer conceals this with his hand and lets someone push a card in the other end of the book; then he turns the book in stepping to another person. In this case any book may be used. But it is inferior to the others.

In the improved method, both the page and word are forced; but in a very clever and mystifying manner.

The performer first procures cards of three colors—say blue, white and yellow. Then he selects a word that appears quite frequently in the book he intends to use, which is an ordinary novel.

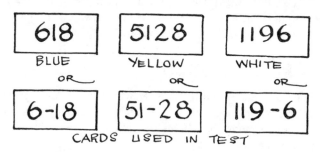

BLUE YELLOW WHITE

OR OR OR

CARDS USED IN TEST

Let us suppose this word appears at 18 on page 6. On a blue card, the magician writes 618. If it appears as word 28 on page 51, he writes 5128 on a yellow card. If it appears at word 6 on page 119, he writes 1196 on a white card. Blue cards where the page number has but one figure; yellow cards for two figure pages; white cards for three figure pages.

Having prepared fifty or sixty cards, all with different numbers, the magician gives these to a person along with the book and retires to a respectful distance.

"Will you select a card?" he asks. "Hold it in your hand but don't let me see the number on it."

A yellow card is lifted.

"Take the first two figures for the page," says the performer. "The remaining pages will give you the word. Count down to that word on the page."

The spectator complies with the request. The word is discovered and it appears on the slate, or is revealed as the performer may choose.

The great variety of numbers on the card will convince everyone that the choice was freely made, especially as a familiar book is used.

It will be noted how this trick works in with spirit effects. The revelation of the chosen word on a slate or in a card on a frame is an effective conclusion; methods of obtaining such results appear later in this book.

SPIRIT TRICKS

One of the most important factors in spirit tricks is obtaining knowledge of what a person has written on a slip of paper. Two specially good methods are presented herewith.

9. THE BEST BILLET SWITCH

The "Billet Switch" is the method by which one folded piece of paper is exchanged for another. Through its use, many fraudulent mediums tell persons the names of their departed friends, and give them other information.

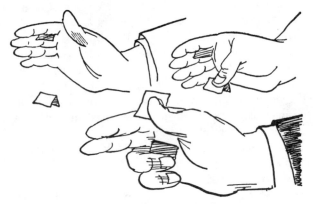

The three movements of the "Billet Switch."

In effect, the performer requests that someone write a name on a slip of paper; fold it and lay it on the table. This is done and the performer tosses the slip into a burner. He seats himself at a table and gazes at the flame or into a crystal ball. Then he tells the name that was on the paper.

Sometimes the same effect is done by the performer holding the slip to his forehead; then replacing it on the table. The spectator receives the slip at the conclusion of the séance, after the performer has revealed the written name.

The whole secret is the substitution of a duplicate billet for the original. This is done so quickly and so easily that most persons will declare the performer never touched the slip of paper.

The slip is folded beforehand and unfolded so that the writer will follow the folds and make the billet the proper size—identical with the duplicate or "dummy" billet which the performer has in his possession.

The duplicate is held between the first two fingers of the right hand, by the edge. The original is set on the table so that it stands like a tiny tent. Holding his hand bent inward, the performer places it over the billet as a shield. He immediately closes his third and fourth fingers, pressing the billet into his hand; and as he raises his hand, his thumb tilts the "dummy" billet so that it appears between his thumb and forefinger.

In practice this movement takes place in the fraction of a second, and it is absolutely indetectible.

He transfers the "dummy" billet to his left hand, and while holding it to his forehead, or burning it, the right hand drops beneath the table and opens the original billet so the performer can read it with a downward glance.

If he chooses to return the slip, the performer refolds it, places the "dummy" on the table and makes the switch again in the action of returning the billet to the sitter.

10. THE INK-BOTTLE

This is another way of getting the desired information from a slip of paper. The magician requests the writer to put the folded message in an empty ink-bottle. It remains there and is removed later on.

The ink-bottle is an imitation, made of wood. It has no bottom. Inside it is a piece of brass tubing. The message goes into the tube. The performer corks the bottle and slides it to the edge of the table with his right hand. The left hand is below the edge, and it catches the tube; or the tube may be dropped into the lap.

Turning away on some pretext—to get a book, or a crystal, or to allow the spectator to concentrate in silence, the performer draws the message from the tube, reads it and puts it back.

Later on he picks up the ink-bottle again, and in lifting it from the edge of the table, pushes the tube back into the bottle.

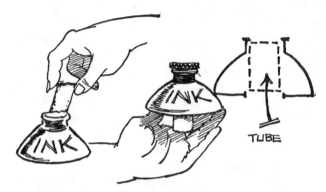

Obtaining the message from the ink-bottle.

In the meantime, of course, he can reveal what was written there, or answer any question written on the paper.

11. THE MYSTERIOUS NAME

This trick is done with a sheet of cigarette paper. The magician rolls the paper into a tiny ball, lays it on the table and asks the spectator to name some famous person. The paper ball is placed upon the tip of a pencil. When opened, it bears the chosen name.

In his trousers pocket the magician has a pad of cigarette papers and a very short pencil. When he has rolled up a blank piece of paper he asks for a famous name. The moment it is given, he puts his hand in his pocket and writes the name on top of the pad with the short pencil; he tears off the slip, rolls it into a wad and conceals it between the tips of his first two fingers.

He brings his hand forth and picks up the slip on the table, adding the other little ball to it. He holds the two as one and turns them over. Everyone supposes that he holds the original ball alone.

In his left hand the magician holds a pencil, point upward.

His right fingers retain the original ball of paper, but set the ball with the written name upon the point.

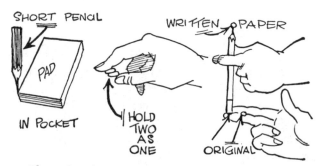

LEFT: The pad in the pocket.
CENTER: Exchanging the pellets.
RIGHT: Concealing the original pellet.

The pencil is of the eraser type: but the rubber is missing. The cavity from which it came is partly filled with wax. The right fingers pass to the bottom of the pencil and it is set upon the hidden ball, which sticks to the wax. With his right hand the magician gives the pencil to a spectator. Then he shows his hands absolutely empty. When the paper ball is opened, the name is written on it—and the magician calmly pockets the pencil!

12. POCKET SLATES

"Spirit Slate Writing" is an old trick. The commonest form of slate has a flap upon it—when the flap is removed, hidden writing appears.

The disposal of the flap is something of a problem at close quarters. The pocket-size spirit slates solve it. They are only three inches long by two inches wide.

The slates are shown blank on both sides. Each slate is wiped with a handkerchief. In wiping the slate with the flap, it is laid on the handkerchief flap-side down. The flap drops in the cloth, and is carried away to the pocket. Then the slates are placed together and the message comes between them. Another method is to merely let the flap fall in the hand.

13. THE ABACUS SLATE

This is a flap slate. A message appears upon it, simply because the flap is allowed to fall on the table behind a book upon which the slate is momentarily stood. But the clever part of the trick is that the message appears in colored chalk—in a color freely chosen by the audience!

The slate is a child's slate with an abacus of two rows above the slate. There are sixteen beads on the abacus, and only four of them are of the color in which the message is written.

Yet when the performer asks a spectator to name any number from 1 to 16, and when he counts to that number on the abacus, he always arrives on the chosen color.

The important point is that he always counts in the regulation manner—top row, left to right; then bottom row, left to right.

The beads are arranged so that the desired color appears at 1, 5, 11, and 15. But if the slate is turned around before counting, these beads will appear at numbers 4, 8, 10, and 14.

If the slate is inverted, the beads will appear at 2, 6, 12, and 16; or at 3, 7, 9, and 13, according to which way the slate is turned. The magician is familiar with the slate. When the chosen number is decided upon, he merely sets the slate in the proper position to count, and he is sure of striking the proper color.

14. THE MECHANICAL SLATES

The mechanical slates are slates upon which two messages appear —one on each slate; yet the slates may be inspected before or after the trick.

A flap is used; but it locks to one slate at the beginning. It covers a message on the slate; also on the underside of the flap.

The slates are tied together. When the performer takes them and holds them above his head, his fingers draw back the ends of the top slate, and the flap is released. His thumbs draw back the ends of the bottom slate, and the flap drops on to it.

When he releases pressure, the ends spring back into position and the flap is locked on the lower slate.

These slates cannot be cheaply made as they must stand fairly close inspection, and their mechanical operation must be exact.

They represent one of the latest developments of this type, and enable the magician to obtain a message without taking the slates out of sight, and without getting rid of anything.

15. THE NUMBER FORCING PACK

When a message is written beforehand on a slate, the magician must be able to force that message on his audience. Forcing packs of playing cards are well-known, the simplest consisting of a pack of cards that are all alike.

But it is much better to use a numbered pack. Then a number, from 1 to 100 may be chosen, apparently at random; or the number may refer to the page of a book, or a certain word on a printed page.

The new type of number forcing pack is unusually clever. Fifty or one hundred cards, numbered consecutively, are shown mixed. Every card bears a different number, plainly stamped in its center. The performer fans the pack and shows all the cards.

Each card has an index corner bearing the number; and a person is allowed to insert a knife in the end of the pack and turn up the card, noting the number. Yet that number is forced!

The simple explanation is that one index corner of every card bears the same number. When the performer fans the pack, this is not observed, because he does not spread that end of the pack. But when the knife is inserted, he sees that it goes into the end where all the numbers are alike.

A card is slightly withdrawn so that the chooser can see the number on the index corner. That is all he sees of the card. It is enough to convince him—and it is enough to do the trick.

16. BLACKSTONE'S PET TRICK

This is a card trick; but it is included in this section as it is a psychic effort, and an unusually surprising one.

The magician lays a pack of cards on the table, and with it a piece of photographic paper measuring about one inch by three-quarters. The paper is examined, and someone is allowed to write his initials upon it. The pack is cut and the paper is laid, initial side up, between the cut portions.

The magician lifts the top portion of the pack and shows the queen of clubs, just above the tiny slip. When the photo paper is turned over, it bears a picture of the queen of clubs! The initials are still upon it, and the person who wrote them is allowed to keep the little card as a souvenir of a real mystery. Here is the secret:

Two slips of paper are used. The performer, in idly shuffling the pack, finds the queen of clubs and slips it to the bottom. Then he lays the pack of cards on the table. The pack is cut before the paper is examined.

Reaching in his pocket he obtains the slip with the photo, and holds it hidden in the bend of the third finger of his right hand. He also brings out an unprepared slip of the same size. This is examined.

The magician picks up the slip and asks someone to write his initials on it. Before anyone can produce a pencil, the magician reaches to his vest pocket and gets one himself. The slip is in his fingers, and he lets it drop into the vest pocket as he brings out the pencil.

Then he carelessly lays the slip that bears the photo with the picture side down. The exchange is so subtle that no one suspects it, especially as the trick has just begun. The initials are written upon it.

The magician calmly lays the slip on the upper portion of the pack, shows his hands empty and asks someone to complete the cut. This naturally brings the queen of clubs on to the slip. When the top portion of the pack is lifted, the queen of clubs is seen; and the photograph is found on the little slip.

The magician should have a supply of these little slips, bearing pictures of different cards so that the result will usually be different.

17. SEALED MESSAGE READING
(*Improved Method*)

The magician passes out small slips of paper, and envelopes. He requests that each person write a question on the slip of paper, sign it and seal it in the envelope. Then he gathers the envelopes in a hat.

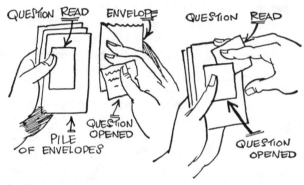

Exchanging the questions in the sealed message reading.

Holding an envelope to his head, he answers the question; opens the envelope, removes the question, reads it aloud and immediately returns it to the writer.

He repeats this with most of the questions, answering each in turn, and returning them all. He also answers a question or two without opening the envelopes containing them, but by returning them to the writers with the request that they open and read them aloud.

This is an excellent mystery, accomplished by very simple means. Based on an old principle, it has certain improvements that deceive those who may know or suspect the old system.

In the explanation, the old way will be given first. The performer has a confederate who writes a question known to the magician. His envelope is marked so the performer will recognize it. The magician picks up any other envelope, and holding it to his head, answers the question in the marked envelope. The confederate acknowledges it. Opening the envelope the magician reads the question aloud from memory, actually reading the writing on the slip.

He picks up another envelope, answers the question he has just read, and opens the envelope when it is acknowledged. In reading it aloud from memory, he learns another question, and he continues thus until he has answered all he desires.

This simple method is very effective. It is used by pretended mediums. The performer can heighten the effect by making a clever pretense of reading when he is talking from memory; he can also turn the questions toward the spectators without giving them time to glimpse them closely; in fact he can make a real mystery of the trick.

But the additional effects to be described improve the trick enormously.

First: The magician has a duplicate slip of paper bearing the confederate's question. This is hidden among some extra envelopes. When he brings back the questions in the hat, he transfers the envelopes above the duplicate question to the bottom of the pile. He keeps the envelopes in his left hand, the question being on top, turned toward him. The papers are smaller than the envelopes. The slip cannot be seen.

He picks an envelope from the hat, holds it to his forehead, and answers the confederate's question. He tears open the envelope, removes the question and pretends to read it, really reading the confederate's question which is lying on the envelopes.

Now he takes the opened envelope between the second and third fingers of his right hand, and the question between his thumb and forefinger.

He places the opened envelope on the bottom of the pile, and the question on top of the pile, all in the same motion. The question is left there; and the thumb and forefinger remove the confederate's question, the left thumb retaining the question placed on the envelope.

Thus the right hand can immediately pass the question to the confederate, and people can see that it is the question just read by the performer.

Taking another envelope from the hat, the performer answers the question which he has on the pile. He opens the envelope and uses the same transfer as before. This enables him to hand the question he has just read to the writer.

He repeats this all the way through, ending with the confederate's marked envelope. So at the finish he has the confederate's question back on the pile again!

In pretending to read questions after he has opened envelopes, the performer has the preceding question in full view so that he will make no mistakes in reading. He reads from the pile—not from the question in his hand.

The effectiveness of this procedure is obvious. No great skill is required to switch the questions. But the performer should not walk among the audience. He should pass the questions to the nearest person. This is because he does not want anyone to see that he has a question on the pile of envelopes.

Now the additional effect is this—the reading of an envelope without opening it.

The magician gives an envelope to the confederate early in the game. While he is still distributing envelopes and gathering sealed ones in the hat, he cautions everyone to sign their name. The confederate in passing his envelope to the performer remarks that he forgot the signature. The performer has just dropped the envelope into the hat. He withdraws it, and hands it to the confederate with a new envelope, telling him to tear open the old one, sign his name to the question, and to seal it in the new envelope.

But in reality he leaves the confederate's envelope in the hat, and gives him someone else's envelope. The confederate opens it, pretends to sign it, and seals it in the new envelope which bears a tiny mark. On the old torn envelope he writes the question that was in the envelope he opened. No one notices this as the confederate is not too close to other people, and all are busy with their own questions.

The assistant throws the sealed envelope into the hat, and hands the performer the torn envelope, writing side down. The performer tosses it on the table, behind some object, such as a book, and lets it fall with the writing up.

He proceeds as usual with his reading. But in course of action he comes to the envelope with the tiny mark. He experiences trouble in answering the question, and in walking around, or sitting at the table, notes the question on the torn envelope.

Finally he asks who wrote the question he is holding, giving a few words of the question as a clue. The person acknowledges the question. The performer gives him or her the envelope and asks the person to concentrate. Then he answers the question. He tells the person to open it and read it aloud. The person does so, and everyone is amazed that the performer has accomplished the feat. This should be done near the end of the readings, and no special significance should be attached to the fact. It merely creates the indelible impression upon the spectators that the performer is answering all the questions before he opens them—and that is just the effect he is after.

With an audience of more than a dozen persons, the performer may employ two confederates, both of whom forget to sign their names. Each one does the same, receiving a specially marked envelope—envelopes with different marks to distinguish them. Their original envelopes are also marked. One is the envelope which the performer reserves till last as it contains the dummy question.

But the performer can now answer three sealed questions at intervals, returning the envelopes unopened. The first is the one "tipped off" by confederate A. The second is the one "tipped off" by confederate B; and the third is the actual question written by confederate B—a question agreed upon by the performer and confederate beforehand.

On the platform, with a large audience, the performer may use more than two confederates; but too many are inadvisable.

In receiving every question in the hat, the performer should ask the writer if he or she signed the question. Most of them will do so, as they are told to beforehand. But occasionally one will forget. In such instances the performer immediately returns the sealed envelope with another envelope asking that the mistake be rectified; and he always collects the torn envelope along with the sealed one—the same procedure that he uses with his confederates. This proves very mystifying.

The answering of questions is an art in itself. Needless to say, when the performer knows the question, as he does in this demonstration, he can make some sort of an answer. But experience will teach him to give some clever answers.

When someone asks concerning a lost article, the clever performer makes an evasive reply yet gets an "impression" that the article is hidden in a bureau drawer, or in an old suit. Very often lost articles are actually found after such a guess.

There are many other types of answers, and special booklets have been compiled on the subject. But it is not the province of this book to cover such details. The author assumes that the reader intends to present the trick as a form of light entertainment, with no pretense of super-human power, but merely with a desire to create an interesting mystery. The mind-reading "profession" has sometimes produced fakers who use trick methods to obtain dupes. Presented purely as magic, these tricks are legitimate and mystifying.

18. TWO SLATE TEST

This is a very simple, but effective method of obtaining a message without the use of flap slates. The performer has two slates set together—one slate being larger than the other. He marks the outside of each slate with a letter X.

Then he opens the slates and shows the insides blank. He puts the slates together with the blank sides outward and marks them with an X.

When the slates are again opened, a message is found on the smaller slate—replacing the letter X that was originally there.

The message is written on the inside of the smaller slate at the beginning. The slates are placed together, the little slate on top. The performer marks this lightly with an X.

Then he turns the slates over; while his right hand marks an X on the large slate, his left fingers rub off the X from the small slate.

Remarking that he will show the insides of the slates, the performer takes one in each hand, the large slate covering the smaller. Under this concealment, the left hand gives the small slate a half-turn; then the slates are opened book-wise.

The half-turn has thrown the writing out of sight—the spectators see the side of the small slate that was originally marked X but which is now quite blank.

The small slate is laid upon the large one, the blank sides outward, and the outer sides are marked. The message is now inside, and is revealed at the proper time.

19. THE FIGURE TOTAL SLATE

The magician has a slate which is divided into five sections by horizontal painted lines. He invites various spectators to write numbers in these sections—all except the bottom section. That space is reserved for the total, which is added by another person.

No matter what numbers are written, the performer knows the total, and can reveal it in some mysterious manner!

An examination of the slate explains how this can be done. A thin metal flap is used—painted black. It is fitted into the sides of the slate, at the second cross line from the top. This flap may be swung back and forth to cover either the two top sections or the third and fourth sections. Both sides of the flap have a white line across the center to correspond with the white line that the flap covers when in position.

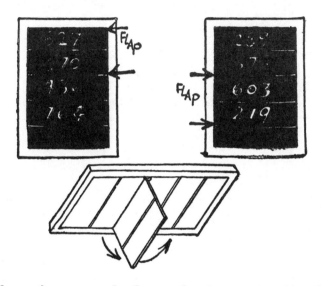

The performer sets the flap so that it covers sections three and four. Then in all four sections he writes numbers, and adds the total, which he remembers. Then he swings the flap so that it covers sections one and two. The result is a blank slate—blank except for the cross lines.

The spectators write their numbers on the slate. The performer turns the slate back upward as he walks to another spectator. This enables him to secretly shift the flap. The result is that the *performer's original figures are added instead of the numbers written by the spectators*. Immediately after the addition the flap is swung back again so that the performer may carelessly show the spectators' numbers. But the total remains in view.

20. CARD AND FRAME MYSTERY

This is an excellent method of revealing a chosen number—a number which is "forced" on the audience by use of the "Figure Total Slate" or some other system.

The performer shows a sheet of cardboard, blank on both sides. He lays it upon a tray and invites some person to write his name upon it.

Then he exhibits a large frame—just large enough to hold the cardboard. The frame contains a sheet of glass, which is quite transparent.

The piece of cardboard is placed against the glass, with the name still showing; it is fastened in position and the front of the frame is shown, with the blank cardboard facing the audience. The frame is set on a special stand and is reversed so the name side of the cardboard again faces the audience.

When the frame is turned around again, the number has appeared on the sheet of cardboard, which is removed from the frame and is given for examination!

The bottom of the frame is hollow, forming a compartment which is filled with white sand. The glass is double—with a thin space between the two layers; and this space connects with the hollow side of the frame.

Two sheets of cardboard are used; one has the number written upon it; the other is painted black on one side to match the tray used in the trick.

These cardboards are shown as one—the inside surfaces being the side with the number and the black side. The magician lays the two sheets upon the tray, and lets the spectator write his name. Then he lifts a single sheet of cardboard. As a result he has the spectator's name on one side, and the number on the other; but he does not reveal the latter side.

After setting the cardboard in the frame, the performer, in clamping it there, carelessly inverts the frame. The sand trickles down into the double glass. Then he can show the face of the cardboard apparently blank—for the sand appears to be the surface of the cardboard.

In putting the frame on the stand, the performer turns the sand side from view, and again inverts the frame. The sand goes back into its secret compartment; and when the face of the frame is shown the number has made its mysterious appearance on the face of the cardboard!

21. FIGURE SWITCHING PADS

An easy method to switch figures is by the use of a small pad. Two types are described here.

(A) Write your own figures on the bottom sheet of the pad.

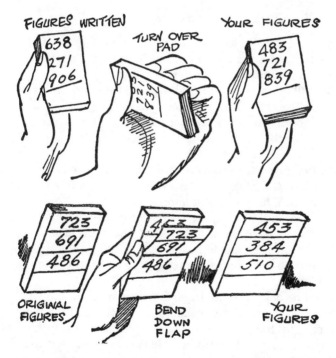

Hold it in your hand while the spectators write their figures on the top sheet. In going to another spectator, calmly reverse the pad, and let him add your figures.

(B) Fold the top sheet of the pad in half—crosswise. Do the same with another sheet, and paste the backs of the folded portions so that they form an inverted T. You thus have a flap which can be swung either way.

Divide both surfaces with four horizontal lines. Put your own figures on one surface; hide it by bending the flap over. Let the spectators write their figures; switch the flap, and let another person add the totals on another pad. Switch back the flap and check up on each person's number; pocket the pad, and proceed with the trick, using the number that the spectator has added—your own total.

22. THE WRIST PILLORY

This is a device which may be used for cabinet manifestations where the performer retires from view and although imprisoned, causes many unusual things to take place.

The pillory is made of wood, divided into two sections, with hasps at the ends. The performer places his wrists in the holes and demonstrates that he cannot remove his hands. Padlocks are attached to the hasps and the performer goes behind a screen, minus his coat, but wearing a vest.

Immediately manifestations take place. His hands clap loudly and his vest is thrown over the screen; yet the performer immediately appears, his wrists still imprisoned.

The holes in the pillory are not centered exactly. One is slightly above center; the other slightly below. The wrists cannot slip free when the pillories are locked in this position. But when he is ready for the test, the performer quietly reverses the top half of the pillory.

Thus one hole becomes large, the other small; as the wrists are in the holes the difference cannot be detected, and the performer can instantly free one hand. This enables him to clap his hands and remove his vest; yet he can immediately get the free hand back into the pillory.

The pillory can be used in full view. The performer's hands are behind his back; yet suddenly a hand emerges and taps a person who is standing beside the performer. The wrists are immediately shown locked as firmly as ever.

23. THE THUMB PILLORY

This is a miniature pillory just large enough for the performer's thumbs. The pillory is locked to the thumbs by means of bolts that run lengthwise through the ends, with wing-nuts on the ends.

LEFT: The thumb pillory as it normally appears.
RIGHT: The pillory with one section reversed. Note variation in size of holes.

The performer asks a person to put his arm between the performer's arms, and to shake hands with another person. The performer then strikes the arm in front of him with his hands; his hands apparently pass through the spectator's arm, and he is free; yet his thumbs are still locked in the pillory!

Large rings are tossed to the performer. He catches each ring on his arm, immediately showing that his thumbs are still locked. Then he gives the rings a toss and they fly free—yet the pillories still hold the thumbs, and the nuts must be removed to free the performer.

The "Thumb Pillory" is identical with the "Wrist Pillory" but on a smaller scale. The reversal of the upper half makes one hole larger than the other, as the holes are not properly centered.

First the performer has his thumbs pilloried in a genuine manner. Before the bolts are fastened with the nuts, he asks that the top section of the pillory be removed. The bolts are in the upper half, and the performer uses the lower half to strike them and show that they are solid. This gives him the opportunity to reverse the lower half.

When he is locked in, he finds that it is but the work of an instant to remove one thumb. He masks this movement by tilting the hands upward and keeping the fingers in front of the pillory.

The instant his hands have passed the spectator's arm on a downward or an upward stroke, they are brought together and the loose thumb is slipped into the hole again.

The same action is used in catching the rings and releasing them. A downward and upward movement covers the slipping of the thumb, and the hands are separated very slightly. The practiced performer can execute this trick with rapidity and precision that escape detection.

24. A RAPPING HAND

There are several versions of the "Rapping Hand Trick," a spiritualistic effect in which a wax or wooden hand answers questions by moving up and down, tapping its fingers in a mysterious manner.

For close work, the most practical method is to have the hand placed upon a board, which is held by the performer during the manifestations. The board appears quite innocent; yet the trick

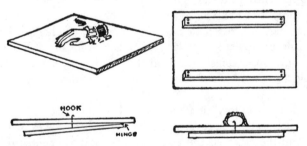

Construction of the board used in the "Rapping Hand." Note action of brace beneath the board.

lies in it; and the particular type of board described here is new, inexpensive to construct, and easy to operate.

The board is about twelve by eighteen inches in size. It is dark in color, with a roughened surface. Midway between the two ends of the board, but only a few inches from the back, is a tiny hole that passes through the board.

Under the board are two braces, each eighteen inches long. One is near the front of the board; the other close to the back, and the latter comes directly beneath the hole near the back of the board.

This brace is hinged at the left end. The other end is loose. Running up from the center of the brace is a stout wire that terminates in a slight hook; it runs through the hole in the board.

The performer gives the hand for examination. He shows the bottom of the board, holding the loose brace pressed against the board with his right hand. The brace is fitted with several short screws which make it appear to be firmly fastened to the board.

After showing the bottom of the board, the performer shows the top. While the board is turning over, the protruding hook will not be discerned, as it is very small and black. The performer then releases the brace beneath the board. It drops about an inch, bringing the tiny hook flush with the surface of the board.

The wooden hand is placed upon the board. It has a cloth binding at the wrist; and as the hand is shifted to the proper position by the performer's left hand, his right hand presses up the brace, and the sharp little hook engages the wrist of the wooden hand.

It is then an easy matter to operate the rapping hand. The brace is pushed down or raised by the performer's right fingers, and it controls the actions of the hand.

By counting each rap a letter of the alphabet the hand can spell names; it can count to "forced" numbers; and it can answer questions "yes" and "no," three raps meaning an affirmative, and two a negative.

The braces do not extend the full length of the board; they are trimmed off slightly, so that they are completely hidden underneath.

CHAPTER FIVE

Stage Magic and Illusions

THE stage magician must use special care in the choice of his magical effects. The tricks he employs must be large enough to be seen at a distance; and for this reason he is forced to omit some very clever smaller effects from his program.

He does, however, have the advantage of distance. He can use certain apparatus that would not be effective at close range, without fear of detection.

Under the head of stage magic come large tricks and illusions, the last named being those effects that involve the appearance, disappearance, or transformation of human beings or large animals.

There are, of course, some stage tricks that can be done on a small platform; just as there are some close-range tricks that will work on the stage. There is no exact dividing line, but a study of each individual trick will show its limitations and its qualifications.

The stage magician usually has the advantage of one or more assistants, so in the description of the effects which follow, the presence of such helpers is understood.

1. PRODUCTION OF FLUIDS

The production of articles from beneath a cloth is customary with most magicians. In this production the performer brings forth a tray with half a dozen small glasses of vari-colored liquids.

Two trays are used—a lower and an upper. The upper tray is cushioned and covered with rubber. The glasses are put on the lower tray, and the upper tray set upon them so that the cushioned rubber side protects the liquid.

A strap passes over both trays, holding them together, and it is designed for easy release. There is a hook on the bottom of the lower tray, which enables the magician to hang it in one of three places: beneath his coat, on his back, or on an assistant's back.

This is an opening production—the magician's first trick. He shows a foulard or cloth on both sides, and drapes it over his extended left arm. Under cover of the cloth, he obtains the trays, which are hanging vertically. He raises them to the horizontal, releases the straps and lifts off the upper tray with the cloth, so that his left hand appears holding the tray with the glasses filled with fluid.

If the apparatus is concealed beneath the coat, the magician can hide any bulkiness by keeping the cloth constantly in the left hand—the side on which the apparatus is placed.

If he has the apparatus on his back, he must constantly face the audience; the cloth over the left arm will hide the right hand as it reaches under the left arm.

If the apparatus is on the assistant's back, the assistant brings in the cloth, and while the magician holds one side in his left hand, and the assistant holds the other, the magician's right hand gets the trays.

2. FLOWER BASKET PRODUCTION

This is a neat production as the apparatus is not bulky. It is a shallow circular tray about six inches in diameter. Projecting upward are several rods, which are connected by horizontal ribbons, giving the effect of a basket.

A quantity of "spring flowers" is placed in the basket; and the upright rods are folded inward. Each one has a spring to force it upward; but they are all held down by a catch on the last rod.

A hook on the bottom of the tray lets it hang beneath the coat, and it takes up very little space.

The cloth is thrown over the left arm. The right hand brings out the tray, holds it horizontal, and pulls the catch. The rods

The open basket appears at the left. The appearance of the basket when collapsed is at the right.

spring up and the compressed flowers fill the basket, making a very nice display when the cloth is removed.

3. LIGHTED LAMP PRODUCTION

This is the production of a lighted lamp on an undraped table. It is an ingenious device that must be carefully constructed. It is hidden in the table.

The lamp consists of a rod which goes down into the table leg. The top of the table is hollowed and it contains the collapsible base of the lamp and the cloth shade, which presses flat. To hide the lamp, a circular piece of black cloth is set over the top of the table.

The magician drapes a large foulard over his left arm and pretends to catch the lamp. He goes to the table, and holds the cloth above it. With his right hand he reaches through a tiny hole in the black cloth that covers the lamp, and grips a hook with his finger, drawing the lamp up from the table leg. When the lamp is fully extended it lights automatically from a flashlight battery in the center rod, and it becomes firm, so when the foulard is removed, the lamp stands on the table.

The black cloth is carried away in the foulard.

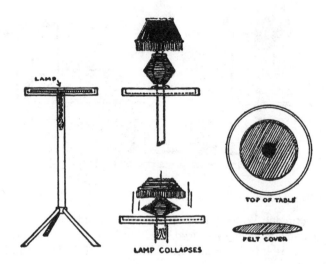

4. THE VANISHING LAMP

A lamp is resting on a tray. The magician places a paper about it, and carries the lamp away. It disappears from the paper.

The lamp is just half a lamp, made entirely of wood. It is at the front of a rectangular tray, which is held lengthways by an assistant.

When he covers the lamp with the piece of paper, and starts to form the tube, the magician knocks the lamp flat. It locks in position when it strikes the tray; and at the same instant the assistant tilts the tray forward.

The tray has three lengthwise panels; the center one is reversible, and the weight of the lamp makes it do a turn on its pivots which are in the ends of the panel.

So as the magician pretends to carry the lamp away, the assistant holds the tray with the top directly toward the audience showing that there is nothing there. The assistant carries away the tray with the imitation lamp hidden on the bottom.

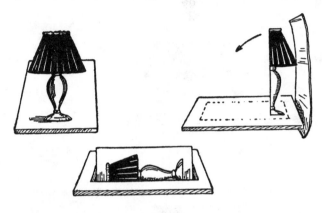

5. THE GERMAINE JARS

The "Germaine Water Jars" have enjoyed considerable fame, but few magicians have ever used the standard sets effectively because the trick in its usual form lacks conviction. The following method is an improvement.

The magician has four jars or vases, each eight inches high and six in diameter. He shows each vase empty and proves that it contains nothing.

He puts two jars side by side, and sets a single jar upside down upon each one. When he lifts each upper jar, he pours a vaseful of water into it, from the jar beneath.

Six jars are used. All are the same size, and they nest snugly; but two are bottomless. When one jar is placed within another they fit so neatly that at stage distance they appear to be a single jar.

The magician also requires two discs of metal, each with an inner ledge. The tops of ten cent paint cans are just right as they have a diameter of slightly less than three inches—the diameter of the bottom of each jar. When one of these discs is set on the table, with the ledge upward, a bottomless jar can be placed upon it, and the disc will act as a temporary bottom, the ledge keeping it in place.

The jars are set as follows, from left to right as the performer sees them:

(A) A single jar.

(B) A single bottomless jar with false bottom in place.

(C) A single jar in a bottomless jar with false bottom in place.

(D) A single jar within a single jar.

Jars C and D (that is, the inner jars) are more than half-filled with water.

A large handkerchief rests on the table in back of the jars.

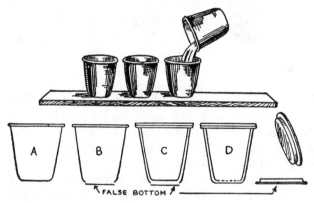

TOP: The Germaine jars as they appear.
BOTTOM: Arrangement of the jars before the trick.

Procedure: The magician shows Jar A empty. He sets it down and shows Jar B empty, by lifting the false bottom with it. Then he replaces Jar B on the table.

To demonstrate that Jar B is really empty, he inserts Jar A in it. He shows Jar A empty again; picks up Jar B and shows it empty.

He palms the disc from the bottom of Jar B, and inserts the jar in Jar C. As soon as it is in, he drops his right hand to the handkerchief on the table and leaves the disc.

Then he apparently removes Jar B from Jar C; but he brings out the solid jar with the original Jar B inside it.

Then he picks up the single Jar C (with its false bottom), shows it empty, palms off the disc, and puts Jar C slowly into Jar D. He lifts the solid jar from Jar D, bringing the bottomless jar within it.

He then picks up Jar D and shows it empty; to complete the circuit he inserts Jar D into Jar A.

He removes Jar D and inverts it on Jar C; he inverts Jar A on Jar B. Then he is ready for the production of the water.

The "patter" shows how natural and convincing the procedure can be.

"Here," says the magician, "are four empty jars, which I shall exhibit one by one. The first jar, you see, is empty.

"The second jar is also empty. Now these jars are all the same size. To prove conclusively that they contain nothing and that no optical illusion is employed, I shall place the first jar—empty—into the second empty jar.

"Obviously the second jar must be empty when it will hold a jar quite as large as itself. It is empty—as you can see.

"You will note that the second empty jar fits into the third empty jar—filling it entirely. And when I show you the third jar, your eyes see that it is empty.

"This third jar fits into the fourth—proving its emptiness; and when I remove it, I show you the fourth jar—empty as ever. To show that the first jar is empty, I complete the chain by inserting the fourth jar.

"On one jar I place another; and invert a second jar upon the jar that remains. Nothing can enter those jars. But while you are watching, something has entered them. We find that this lower jar is filled with water—and that this lower jar also contains the same fluid."

6. BLACKSTONE'S THREE CARD TRICK

"Three Card Monte"—on a giant scale.

The magician has an easel and three giant cards—two jacks of spades and a queen of hearts.

He lays the cards face down on the easel. Everyone sees where the queen is—but when the cards are reversed, the queen has changed position.

This is repeated with astounding results, as will be explained in the routine. First let us study the construction of the cards.

Each card can be transformed from a queen to a jack or vice versa by a very simple process. The face of the card is divided into thirds—crosswise. One end has a picture of a jack; the center is neutral; the other end shows a queen.

The center is raised, forming a slide or shallow tunnel. A piece of cardboard, two-thirds as long as the card, fits into this tunnel. One half represents a jack; the other half a queen. This device slides back and forth and with its aid both ends of the card appear to be either jack or queen as required.

The edges of the card are raised—like the molding of a tray, so that the slide travels a regular route and goes just the right distance.

Now if a jack is turned sideways in showing the back, it will remain a jack. If it is turned end over in reversing it, the slide will operate automatically and silently, and the jack will become a queen.

Each card is backed with cardboard that resembles the back of a playing card. An ordinary card of normal size may be inserted in the back of one of the giant cards, and allowed to project. This is for a purpose to be described.

The Routine: The magician begins with two jacks and a queen. He mixes them a bit, with the backs to the audience; then shows where the queen is and turns all cards face front.

He puts the queen in the center. In reversing the cards, he transforms the queen into a jack and one of the jacks into a queen. Then he moves the cards about, and asks where the queen is.

Everyone has followed the movements, and a chorus tells him

where the queen is located. But when the face of the card is shown, it is *not* the queen.

The magician reverses the cards again, transforming the queen to a jack and a jack to the queen. Then he picks up an ordinary playing card—a queen of hearts—and states that he will attach it to the back of the big queen. But he attaches it to the card which has now become the queen—not to the card which people suppose is the queen.

The changing cards used in "Giant Three Card Monte."

As he mixes the cards, everyone is sure they know the ruse. They are positive that the card with the little card attached is not the queen—but it proves to be the queen!

For the finale, the magician removes the tiny card and reverses the large cards, changing the queen into a jack—so that he has three jacks and no queen. He asks the audience to point out the queen. When a card is chosen, he shows that it is a jack.

He reverses that card, changing it into a queen and uses it as a pointer to indicate the cards on the easel.

"One of those," he says, "must be the queen. Which is it?" Opinions will differ. While the argument is in process the magician places the card he holds (now the queen) between the two on the easel. Taking one of those two cards in each hand, he shows their faces—and lays them on the easel. The spectators are astonished when they see that both cards are jacks. Then the magician shows the face of the center card, and reveals it as the missing queen!

7. THE NEW SWORD CABINET

This is a real novelty—an improvement on illusion which has been exposed at carnivals and side-shows; an improvement which will bewilder those who think they know how it is done.

In the old trick, the magician has a box mounted on four legs. A door opens at the front, and a girl enters. The door is shut, and the magician pushes a pole through the top of the cabinet and out the bottom. Then he inserts cavalry swords through the sides of the box. This proves—supposedly—that the girl has left the cabinet; but when the swords and pole are removed, she emerges from the box.

In exposing the trick, the top is opened, and people are allowed to look in. They see that the swords run about the girl's body, between her arms and legs, without harming her. So the secret of the illusion, through cheap exposure, has become rather well known.

But in the new cabinet, the magician, after he has started to remove swords and has taken them from the front door, suddenly opens the door of the cabinet—and shows it to be unmistakably empty—except for the swords that criss-cross the interior, and the pole in the center! Then he closes the door, removes the remaining weapons, and the girl comes from the cabinet.

The base of the cabinet is several inches in depth. When the door is closed on the girl, she goes to the back of the cabinet, and through a triangular hole, slips her legs into the double bottom, her body being at the back of the cabinet.

At the sides of the cabinet are two mirrors. When the pole is inserted, the girl pulls the mirrors inward and their edges meet the pole. The mirrors and the back of the cabinet form a triangular space that hides the girl.

Swords are pushed in the sides, but they turn in front of the mirrors. The swords that go in the back point downward, alongside of the girl so they do not reach the backs of the mirrors.

When the front of the cabinet is opened, the box appears to be empty because the mirrors reflect the side of the cabinet and make them appear to be the back. The presence of the pole hides the edges of the mirrors.

The side swords are reflected, and give the appearance of swords through the back. The cabinet can be turned around while the door is opened.

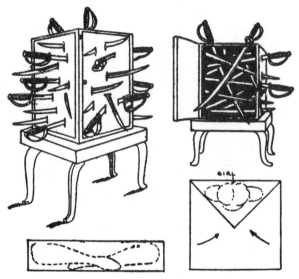

The cabinet before and after the vanish. The diagrams show the girl's legs in the platform and her body at the back.

When the door is closed, the swords are removed, the girl pushes the mirrors against the sides, and when the pole is taken out, she resumes her original position in the center of the cabinet.

To present this illusion properly, the magician should proceed exactly as though doing the old sword cabinet; and he should emphasize the fact that the girl cannot possibly be in the box with the pole and the swords there. Then pretending to hear someone say that he cannot open the door; the magician should remove the swords from the front and throw the door open.

8. THE GLASS TRUNK

A large trunk, mounted on a wheeled platform, is brought on the stage and is shown on all sides. The magician lifts back the

lid, removes the tray, and drops down the front of the trunk, showing that it is empty. Sheets of plate glass are inserted on all sides of the trunk; the tray is replaced; the trunk is closed, and is revolved. When it is opened again, a girl is inside.

The back of the trunk contains a panel, which is hinged to tip forward into the trunk. Set at right angles to the panel is a similar panel, which extends to the back. Thus when the front panel is tilted forward into the bottom of the trunk, the extending panel comes up and forms the back of the trunk.

At the outset, the panel is tipped forward, and the girl is placed in the trunk, which is then wheeled on the stage. After the trunk has been turned with the front toward the audience, the lid is opened and the girl throws her weight to the rear, tipping the foremost panel up to form the back of the trunk, and leaving her outside at the back, resting on the rear panel which forms a temporary shelf.

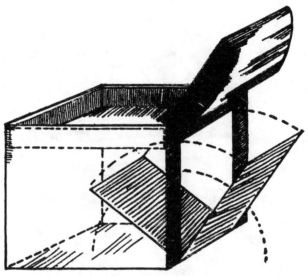

Diagram showing the action of the back panel of the trunk.

No one can see inside the trunk because of the tray. No one can see the girl because she is beneath the lid of the trunk. No one can see up under the trunk, because the platform is thick enough and low enough to cut off the angle of vision.

The tray is then removed, having served its purpose, hiding the transit of the girl; then the front is let down and the sheets of glass are inserted. No glass is placed on the bottom, but one may be placed on the top—where the tray was originally.

As soon as the tray is replaced and the front of the trunk is closed, the girl tips herself inside the trunk. The sheet of glass at the rear is brought between the forward panel and the bottom of the trunk. Then the lid of the trunk is closed. When the trunk is opened again, there is the young lady.

The trunk is wheeled off the stage before the audience suspects that there is no longer a sheet of glass at the rear. This is such a small detail that it is never noticed.

9. A MAGICAL APPEARANCE

This is used as an opening to a magical entertainment. A large four-fold screen is standing on the stage. Two assistants are be-

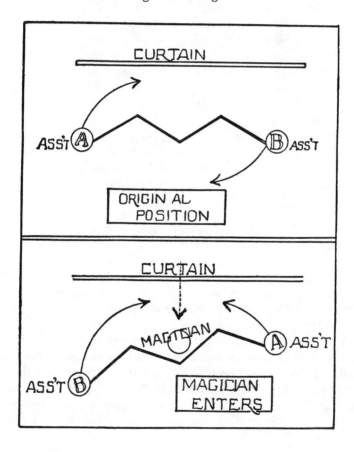

side it. One takes each end of the screen, and they walk in a circle, showing both sides of the screen. Then they form the screen into a square, with the opening toward the rear, and slide it up to the front of the stage, on to a carpet or cloth which has been shown and laid there. A flash of light follows, and the screen opens revealing the magician.

This illusion is very simple, but very effective. It is usually shown with a "drop" or curtain well forward from the back of the stage. There is a secret opening in the curtain—like a panel. In turning the screen around, the assistants carry it back close to the curtain, and the magician comes out in back of it. The assistants fold the screen around the magician, and slide it front and center, ready for the climax.

The magician may also come in from the side of the stage— from the "wing"—in this case the assistants temporarily overlap the wing in showing the screen. He may also come in from behind some piece of apparatus standing on the stage, or from a screen at the side of the stage.

The important factor of the appearance is that the assistants should do their work smoothly and with precision, making the screen into a square the moment that the performer is in position.

10. THE CLEAVER ILLUSION

This is a rather recent development of the torture type of illusion, in which the magician apparently injures an assistant yet does not harm her.

"Sawing a Woman in Two," and other illusions of that sort gained widespread popularity several years ago, and the "Cleaver Illusion," while quite as spectacular as any of them, appeared too late to gain the fame it deserved.

A long box is used in the illusion. The box is divided into seven cross sections, by slits in the sides of the box. The top of the box is also formed by seven separate lids, with spaces between them.

Above the box hangs a rectangular frame, slightly larger than the box, but not larger than the shallow platform on which the box rests. Double-handled cleavers run across the frame. So when the frame is lowered, each cleaver enters a slit and goes completely to the bottom of the box, where the frame rests upon the platform.

The magician demonstrates this by closing the lids of the box and letting the frame go down, under the control of a rope which passes over a pulley.

The ends of the box are opened, so that the spectators may see the action of the cleavers. Then the iron frame is raised, and a girl lies down in the box.

The cover and the ends are closed. The magician slowly lowers the iron frame; and just as the cleavers are inside the box, he "accidentally" drops the rope holding the frame. The cleavers come down with a crash. The iron frame falls against the platform, and surrounds the box. The girl has apparently been killed. But when the magician pulls up the rope, out come the cleavers; the frame is tied up, and when the box is opened, the girl rises, uninjured. How is it done? Very easily!

The cleavers have wooden handles, and those handles slide down into the slits in the sides of the box, so the cleavers themselves are hidden from view when the box is closed. When the girl is in the box, she moves two long shafts, which are at the bottom of the box. The walls of the box are quite thick, and they are hollow. In the walls are vertical rods, attached to the horizontal shafts at the bottom; and at the top of the vertical rods are short horizontal rods. So when the girl pushes the long horizontal shafts lengthwise, the short horizontal rods fill the slits in the sides of the box, just a short distance below the top of the box. The explanatory illustration makes the operation clear. It shows the entire apparatus.

The metal cleavers are not attached to the wooden handles. They simply rest in place. As soon as the big metal frame comes on a line with the short rods in the sides of the box, the rods catch the cleavers and hold them suspended; while the frame and the handles of the cleavers continue to the bottom of the box. The handles of the cleavers are partially in the slits at the sides of the box; so no one can note the absence of the blades, which are entirely within the box.

The girl is perfectly safe beneath the cleavers as they are held firmly in position. Yet to all appearances, the cleavers have dropped to the bottom of the box.

The raising of the frame is done slowly and regularly; the handles of the cleavers, in coming upward, engage the blades and bring them out. This pick-up is automatic.

The proper construction of the box is important, as the blades must be held in exact position, so that the handles will pick them up instantly.

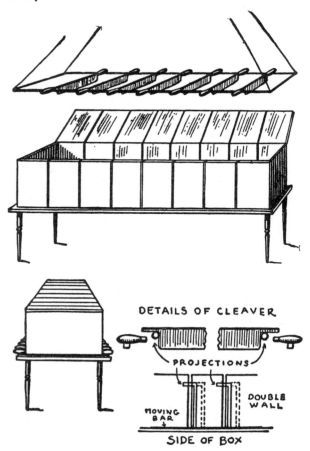

DETAILS OF CLEAVER

PROJECTIONS

DOUBLE WALL

MOVING BAR

SIDE OF BOX

The illusion should also be presented with proper precaution. The magician should be sure that the safety rods are in place, and should not let the frame fall until he has lowered it to a position where the rods have engaged the blades of the cleavers.

11. WALKING THROUGH GLASS

"Walking Through Glass" is the modern development of an illusion performed by the late Alexander Herrmann, which was called "Vanity Fair."

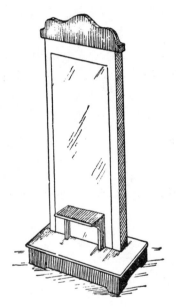

The apparatus.

A sheet of glass, about eight feet high and three feet wide, is set permanently in a frame, which is mounted upon a base. About a foot from the bottom of the glass is a little platform, which extends upon both sides of the sheet of glass. Solid rods connect the platforms with the base beneath, but there is glass beneath the platforms, between the rods.

The solidity of the glass is demonstrated, and a girl stands behind the glass, looking through. A screen is placed about her; and another screen is placed around the platform in front.

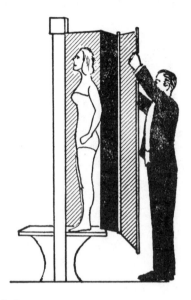

Girl in back of glass.

Now the audience can see glass above, below, and on both sides of the screens. The solid wall of glass is between the screens. Yet when the screens are taken away, the girl is on the front platform, having apparently passed right through the sheet of solid glass.

The glass beneath the platform, and between the rods is a separate piece in itself. The large sheet of glass is movable, and slides up into the frame.

Since the solid sheet does not pass below the platform in the center, but goes down on each side, it is obvious that a rectangular piece must be cut out of the bottom of the sheet of glass—although the spectators do not know it.

As soon as the screens are in place, the girl slides up the sheet of glass, and it goes into the top of the frame a foot or more, the top of the frame being fashioned to receive it. Thus the girl forms an opening, through which she can pass her body.

Girl passes through the glass.

The motion of the glass is not noticeable. If the bottom of the frame is made quite deep, and solid, the sheet of glass can be made so long that the bottom edges will not come into view. In some cases, the bottom of the frame has been made shallow, and the performer and his assistant, by standing at the sides of the front screen, hide the bottom edge of the glass with their legs.

If the girl lifts the glass herself, it is essential to have a safety catch or some similar arrangement to hold the glass up while she goes through the hole. To eliminate the danger and delay necessitated by such a procedure, a lifting device is sometimes used beneath the stage. Two rods, projecting up through holes in the stage press up the lower edge of the sheet of glass, and an assistant raises and lowers the contrivance by means of a lever, when he receives his cue from the magician above.

"Walking Through Glass" was originally presented with a mirror

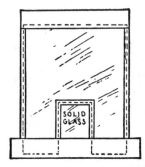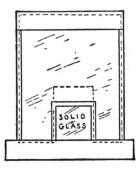

How the glass is raised in the frame.

in the old "Vanity Fair" illusion, and was used as a method of disappearance, the lady going through the mirror from the front, and off the stage on a little bridge connecting with the back curtain.

12. PIGEON, RABBIT, AND GOOSE

In this surprising illusion, the magician has a frame-work mounted on legs. The frame is about thirty inches square. In addition, he shows three sheets of paper, each mounted on a light frame, thirty inches square.

The sheets of paper are shown on both sides. Then they are placed upon a chair. The first sheet is placed on the heavy framework, and with his hands, the magician shows the shadow of a pigeon on the paper.

Breaking the paper, he produces a live pigeon through the paper.

The second sheet of paper is put in position; this time the shadow image of a rabbit is thrown upon it; and the magician breaks the paper to produce a live rabbit.

After the torn sheet is taken away, the third paper is put in the frame-work. The magician forms the shadow of a goose, and breaking the paper, produces a live goose.

The frames that hold the sheets of paper are quite unprepared; the secret lies partly in the large frame-work, and partly in the chair.

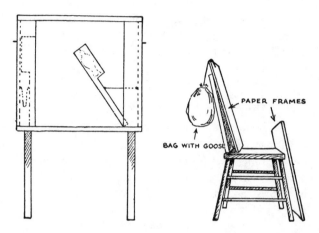

Each side of the frame is hinged at the bottom, so that a strip of the side will swing inward. At the top of each side is a container—one holding a rabbit; the other a pigeon.

The first piece of paper is shown on both sides as it is set upon the frame-work. In fixing it in position, an assistant releases a catch and lets the side of the frame-work fall inward. A heavy cord stops it when it has reached an angle of forty-five degrees, and the container, with the pigeon, is directly behind the center of the paper.

The magician makes the pigeon shadow; breaks the paper, and pulls the pigeon from the container, which is open at the front. As he carries the pigeon forward, the assistants remove the paper; but just before doing so, one assistant draws the rod and container back to the side of the frame-work, where the container locks in place.

The same procedure is used for the production of the rabbit; on this occasion, the second container is allowed to fall.

On the back of the chair is a bag containing a goose. It is affixed to a piece of wire which extends over the back of the chair. When the third paper is lifted, the top of its frame engages the wire, and the goose is carried out of sight behind it. This is not suspected, as the paper was shown on both sides prior to placing it on the chair; and the movement is done in a natural manner.

The frame is set in position; the magician makes the shadow of the goose; breaks the paper and pulls a "zipper" cord in the bag. This releases the goose instantly, and it is produced through the torn paper.

13. THE GIRL AND THE SHADOW

This is an unusual illusion. A light cabinet is used, the walls, back and door being covered with cloth. There is a hole in the top of the cabinet for the insertion of an electric light, and the cabinet stands two feet above the stage, on legs.

A girl enters the cabinet, and the door is closed. The electric light is inserted through the hole, which is near the back of the top; and the stage lights are turned out.

The front of the cabinet is so thin that everyone can see the shadow of the girl through the door. The magician asks her if she is ready to go.

She raises her arms, and answers "Yes."

At that instant, the stage lights turn on; the door is flung open, and the girl has disappeared. The cabinet is shown on all sides, and is finally taken apart and carried off the stage.

The cloth front of the cabinet is double and in between is a flat piece of cardboard cut to resemble the girl. It throws a perfect shadow of the young lady. The arms are hinged, and can be raised by a cord that goes through the top of the door and down the side.

The back of the cabinet is hinged; and the platform has a ledge upon which the girl can stand.

The girl enters the cabinet, and immediately takes her position on the back, by swinging its two sections inward, and bringing them back again. This action is unknown to the audience.

The light is put in the top of the cabinet, and is turned on. Then the stage lights are extinguished. The shadow of the girl is seen immediately; but as all the light is in the cabinet, the girl merely steps from the platform and walks off to the near-by wing.

Showing the effect of the shadow illusion; the panel through which the girl escapes and the form in the front door.

An assistant pulls the cord to make the shadow move. He is standing at one side of the cabinet, the magician at the other. The girl answers the magician from the wing—her voice seems to come from the cabinet. On go the stage lights, and the cabinet is shown empty.

CHAPTER SIX

Selected Secrets

THESE tricks have been specially chosen from many which have come into popularity over a long period of years. Still more could have been included in this section, if novelty or workability had been the only reasons for their choice.

But variety has been sought as an additional factor with the tricks that follow. In looking for something different, the practical magician may find it here. As mentioned elsewhere, novelty is the point that most impresses an audience today. The tricks that follow will provide that feature.

1. THE EGG AND FAN

Once the feature of a fantastic show of wizardry presented by a performer in oriental make-up, this amazing feat has worked its way into the repertoires of more and more magicians until today it has become a standard effect. Its use, however, is still limited, for a reason that will be explained.

The magician takes a small square of tissue paper, wads it into a tiny ball, and places it upon an oriental fan which he holds unfolded and outstretched. To the strains of oriental music or the recitation of a Hindu chant he shakes the fan up and down, back and forth, the wad of paper bouncing in accordance with the motions.

Gradually, yet visibly, the wad of paper takes on an oval shape. Before their eyes they see it become a full-sized egg, which the magician lifts from the fan, holds up for all to see, and finally cracks on the edge of a glass, dropping the contents of the egg within the glass itself to prove it entirely genuine.

Special preparation is required to produce this bizarre effect. That preparation involves the egg itself. Oddly, it is a genuine egg that appears upon the fan, but with certain reservations.

First, an egg is blown. Tiny holes are punched in each end and, by blowing through one, the contents of the egg are forced out the other. Next, the hollowed egg is filled with vinegar, one hole being plugged. The egg is left in this condition overnight. The hole is then unplugged to release the vinegar.

The shell can then be broken away, leaving the lining or inner skin of the egg intact. When deflated, this pliable egg can be wadded to pass as a crumpled bit of paper. It is lying beside the fan when the magician begins the trick by picking up a small sheet of tissue paper and folding or squeezing it into a tight ball.

He holds the paper wad in his left hand while his right picks up the fan, bringing the deflated "egg" with it. The magician then apparently drops the wadded paper in his right hand so that his left can take the fan.

Actually he retains the wad in his left hand along with the fan, while his right displays the crushed lining of the egg. The left hand spreads the fan and the right drops the "wad" upon it. From then on it is a mixture of skill and showmanship. The right hand takes the fan and bounces the wadded ball upon it. Gradually the special egg inflates to its full size. All that remains is to prove it to be the genuine article.

That is easily managed.

In his left coat pocket the magician has a genuine egg. While he is walking about and holding attention with the bouncing fan he obtains the egg from his pocket, at the same time disposing of the original wad of paper. The magician conceals the real egg in his left hand until the "egg" on the fan is fully inflated.

Then the left hand sweeps the egg from the fan, actually crushing it and retaining the deflated skin in the bend of his left fingers, while he displays the real egg in its stead. This egg is broken and its contents dropped into a handy glass.

In picking up the fan to put it aside, the deflated egg skin goes with it. Care should be used in its handling to keep it intact for use in another show.

2. THE NEEDLE TRICK

Years ago, side-show performers specialized in a stunt called the "Hindu Needle Trick," in which the demonstrator placed a dozen or more needles in his mouth, along with a length of thread, and pretended to swallow them.

Later, reaching into his mouth, he would find the end of the thread and draw it out with the needles threaded all along its length. Some performers increased the effect by using as many as fifty needles, but the trick, when it became popular in vaudeville, still resembled a carnival pitch more than an artistic presentation.

The secret lay in switching the original set of needles for a duplicate lot already threaded. The threaded group was concealed in the right side of the mouth, high between the gum and cheek. The unthreaded needles were placed openly on the tongue, which pushed them up above the left gum as soon as the mouth was closed.

The performer than faked a swallowing action. He placed a wadded thread in his mouth and actually swallowed it. The tongue brought the threaded needles down from their hiding place; with his fingers the performer found the end of the thread and drew it slowly into sight with the needles dangling from it.

Aside from its artistic lack, the needle trick is dangerous if improperly handled and therefore should be presented only by performers of long practice and experience, if at all. It has been described here for the reader's information and also as prelude to another and much more modern effect entitled:

3. MYSTIC RAZOR BLADES

Here the magician introduces half a dozen razor blades, each separately wrapped and tucked in slits of a display board that measures about nine inches in length and four inches in height. The slits run lengthwise along the center of the board and each is large enough to receive a packaged blade quite easily.

The blades are unwrapped one by one and each is carefully inserted in the slit nearest to the magician, so that the blades form a little group or clump. Now the magician draws a length of thread from a spool, places the thread in his mouth, and pretends to swallow it.

Next he takes the razor blades, places them upon his tongue, and feigns another swallow. Now from between his lips he draws the thread, and the blades are seen strung along it, all at even intervals!

Actually the blades are tied along the thread, a detail which applies to the old "Needle Trick" as well. But the new "Razor Blade" version, despite its highly dangerous appearance, is practically foolproof.

To begin with, the magician uses special blades that have merely been stamped from the original metal sheets but never sharpened. Also, the switch from one set of blades to the other takes place before the first group is placed in the mouth, not afterward. Actually the harmless blades are in the mouth only briefly.

The switch is made by the display board. It is made of cardboard and is really a double board, the two sections being joined at the top so that it resembles a small easel, shaped like an inverted V (Λ). But the magician always shows it flat, the two segments being pressed together. The hinge along the top is simply a loose, ornamental cloth, matching the binding that runs around the edges of the board, giving it an innocent appearance indeed. A hinge and binding of smooth plastic can be neatly applied to look like part of the board itself.

The back section of the double board is also equipped with longitudinal slits. In the end slit nearest the performer is a batch of six unsharpened razor blades, already threaded. The thread is tied through the center opening and around the end of the front blade. It is then tied to the next blade in the same fashion, allowing some slack between, and so on with the remaining blades.

The slack can be wound loosely about the blades themselves,

as that end of the blades is inserted in the slit, so that the thread remains completely hidden. In fact, the whole duplicate portion of the double board is hidden, as it occupies the upper side of the lower half, thus being concealed within the V fold.

By simply giving the board a backward tilt, the upper half can be flipped over, bringing the lower section into sight. The thumb can expedite this action, and the sections are immediately pressed together between thumb and forefinger so that the appearance of the board remains the same. This is done after the original blades have been tucked in the end slot, so that the duplicate set, coming into sight, appears to be the same.

The action is somewhat like that with the "Figure Total Slate,"* but in this case the entire front half of the "board" is the flap and goes completely over. Perfect misdirection is provided as the performer, holding the board in his left hand, reaches in front of it with his right, to pick up the spool of thread. The right arm hides the flipping action, which can be further covered by a slight turn of the body, putting the left hand briefly but entirely out of the audience's sight.

4. VANISHING WATER

A clever and surprising effect, this is performed with a pitcher of water and a paper cone. Openly and visibly the magician pours water into the cone and holds it carefully so that the contents do not spill, while he sets aside the pitcher.

The magician advances with the water-filled cone, gives it a sudden toss, and catches it. The paper is unrolled and is entirely empty, every drop of the water having vanished!

As a follow-up effect the cone can be formed again. Holding the cone in one hand, the magician pretends to catch water from the air and throw it into the cone. The other hand picks up the pitcher, the cone is lifted above it, and the water, mysteriously returned to the cone, is poured into the pitcher.

The cone has a lining made of transparent celluloid or plastic.

* The Figure Total Slate is described in Chapter IV, page 120.

This lining is also provided with a thin but strong wire hook, or even a stout strip of plastic, curved hook-fashion. In either case the hook projects upward above the edge of the paper cone.

After filling the cone with water the magician lowers the pitcher with his right hand and turns his right side toward the audience. The cone is held in the left hand, and as the magician steps toward a table he brings the pitcher up in front of the cone, brushing it as the pitcher passes.

The rear edge of the pitcher engages the hook and brings the lining out of the cone, water and all, but, being transparent, the lining remains unseen behind the glass sides of the pitcher, which is placed on a table or a tray held by an assistant.

All that remains is for the magician to step forward warily with the cone, keeping up the pretense that it contains water, until, with a surprise flick he opens the cone and shows the water vanished.

To bring the water back: Form the cone anew and pretend to catch water from the air. Turn to the pitcher, pick it up, and bring the cone up behind it, lifting off the hooked lining. The pitcher should be lowered simultaneously with the other hand, the moves synchronizing perfectly.

The cone is raised well above the pitcher, then lowered slowly so the water can be poured back visibly and dramatically. This requires considerable rehearsal but is highly effective.

5. VANISHING MILK

In this effect a quantity of milk disappears from a paper cone, but the trick is practically automatic and can be done anywhere, even while surrounded by spectators. As with the water trick, the milk is first poured from a pitcher into a cone and that is where the deception occurs.

The pitcher is a tall type that bulges slightly, having a shoulder near the top. Within the pitcher is an inner lining of transparent celluloid or plastic. This lining is shaped like a cylinder with a solid bottom. At one point of the top edge the lining has a slight inward bend, widening the gap between the lining and the pitcher. This gap is kept toward the front of the pitcher.

Beforehand: With the aid of a little funnel poked down into the gap the performer fills the space between pitcher and lining with a quantity of diluted milk. This gives the impression that the pitcher is really filled.

When the milk is "poured" into the cone, none comes from the pitcher. Instead, it pours back, so to speak, from the space around the lining into the pitcher proper. The pouring illusion is perfect, the decreasing level of the milk causing spectators to think the cone has been filled. All that remains is to whip open the cone in dramatic style.

To bring back the milk: The magician has a tall glass with a loose celluloid lining, which is provided with a loop of thin wire projecting above it. This lining is filled with milk and "planted" in the milk pitcher before the trick. The milk around the sides of the pitcher hides the fake.

The magician shows a handkerchief and drapes it over the edge of the pitcher while he picks up the empty glass. In lifting the handkerchief, his fingers engage the wire loop and bring up the milk-filled fake, which is loaded into the glass under cover of the handkerchief.

Still covered, the glass is placed on a pedestal. The wizard performs the usual vanish of the milk from the cone and lifts the hanky to show the milk mysteriously arrived in the glass.

6. NEW CLING CLANG

For many years, magicians have presented a "sucker" version of the "Egg Cling Clang,"* in which the fake, or hollow, egg is deliberately exposed in the course of the trick. The magician then proceeds to repeat the "change" of silk to egg, this time finishing by breaking the egg to prove it genuine!

This required a switch of the fake egg for the real, but now an ingenious invention has made the whole effect practically self-

---

* One method of the old "Cling Clang" is given in Chapter II, page 63.

contained. This consists of an imitation egg made of plastic, which opens in the center, box-lid fashion. One section of the egg also has a dividing wall, so that the end forms a separate compartment. That end of the egg has a three-quarter-inch hole drilled in it.

To perform: The magician reaches in his pocket and brings out a small silk handkerchief, holding the egg concealed beneath it. He works the silk between his hands, poking it into the hollow end of the egg.

After showing that the silk has become an egg, the magician lets his thumb expose the hole. Apologetically he explains the trick, saying the egg is a hollow imitation. He then "repeats" the trick to show just how it works. But this time, for the climax, he pretends to break the egg on the edge of a glass tumbler.

Beforehand, the main compartment of the fake has been filled with the contents of a real egg. Being snug and absolutely watertight, the fake can be handled safely in that condition. Now, in "breaking" the egg, the magician spreads the sections and the contents drop into the glass, giving the impression that the egg has become a real one.

7. INSTANT GLASS PRODUCTION

This produces a highly startling effect. The magician shows a large napkin back and forth, suddenly reaches beneath it, and brings out a tall glass filled with water, which can be handed to the audience for immediate inspection.

The trick must be set up just before presentation. On the end of a double loop of string is a ring of transparent celluloid, large enough to slide up the slightly tapering sides of the glass almost to the top.

The end of the loop is wound around a vest or suspender button. The glass is inserted in the ring and is then placed in the left hip pocket, the loop stretching just about that far. When ready for the actual production the glass is secretly lifted from the pocket but is held in position by pressure of the left arm through the coat.

The napkin is displayed back and front, the right hand supplying a crisscross sweeping motion. The left arm releases pressure, the magician makes a slight turn, and the glass swings out from under the coat and up beneath the cloth, where one hand catches it through the handkerchief and the other comes up beneath to grip the glass itself.

While the inner hand holds the glass near the top, the outer hand peels the cloth downward, carrying away the transparent ring, which is stuffed in the left hip pocket with the handkerchief. At the same time the loop is drawn taut and unseen beneath the coat.

8. QUICK JELL

A colored liquid is poured into a tall, tapering glass. The magician places his hand over the mouth of the glass and inverts the latter deftly, so the liquid does not escape. He recites mystic words which he claims will produce a "quick jell" process. He lifts the glass from his hand and the liquid remains there, completely solidified in the form of a cone!

This trick is both neat and easy. The glass has a watertight inner lining in the shape of a transparent plastic cone. In his hand, the magician has a disk or cap of similar material which fits snugly over the open mouth of the conical inner lining.

The magician secretly fixes the cap in place, inverts the glass, and lifts it, showing the "jelled" liquid. This can be carried off on a tray, unless the magician prefers to reverse the process, placing the glass over the jell, turning it right side up, and secretly detaching the cap. The liquid may then be poured from the glass.

Before—and after—the effect, the cap can be attached to the base of the goblet, which is of the stemmed type, thus enabling the magician to show his hands empty.

9. SPOOFY GLASS VANISH

The magician introduces a small tray with a deep cloth drape hanging in front of it. On the tray he places a glass of milk, which he covers with a metal cylinder. He slides the cylinder along the tray, makes a magic pass, and lifts the tube, showing that the glass has vanished.

As the magician sets the tube on a table he makes the mistake of turning the tray around. The amused audience sees the "vanished" glass dangling in a net attached beneath the tray. The lack of drapery in back has given the trick away so the magician becomes a good sport and explains it all.

He shows a hole in the tray where the glass dropped through into the net. He repeats the trick, but this time keeps the tray frontward. After showing the cylinder empty and laying it aside he adds: "But some people still may want to see what's under the tray, so this time we'll show them!" He pulls the drape away; the net is empty. The glass has really gone!

The glass is simply a plastic cylinder, painted white almost to the top to make it appear full of milk.* The tube is double with a space between its outer and inner walls, open at the bottom but closed at the top, so it can be slid down over the supposed glass. The tube may then be shown empty by turning the top end toward the audience.†

The first time the magician lets the glass drop through the trap into the network beneath the tray. The second time he retains it in the cylinder, which is shown "empty" before the climax.

10. RING ON WAND

This trick in its modern form represents a combination of deft timing with perfect misdirection. The magician passes two items for examination: a plain wand and a simple finger ring. He drops the ring down over the wand a few times to show that it slides easily; then, clutching the center of the wand with one hand, he asks a spectator to hold the ends.

All the while, the magician is showing the ring in his free hand.

---

* This "glass" is identical with the "fake" used in the "Mysterious Penetration" described in Chapter II, page 64, but is of fairly stout material.

† Identical with the tube used in "Handkerchief and Glass Production," Chapter II, page 62, but here the tube is used for a vanish.

He strikes the wand—"One, two, three"—and whips his hand away. There is the ring, spinning on the center of the wand, which is left in the spectator's hands for full examination!

Two rings are used. The duplicate is held in the curve of the lower left fingers so it can be slid up over the wand. First, though, the wizard holds the original ring at the tip of his left thumb and forefinger and drops it over the wand, which is held upright by the right hand.

In dropping, the ring is delayed by the right hand, which then lets the ring's fall continue. Now the wand is transferred to the left hand which secretly slides the duplicate ring up to the center. The right drops the original ring down over the wand and it is trapped by the left fingers, which let the duplicate fall instead.

Immediately the left hand fists the wand and holds it horizontally, inviting a spectator to grip the ends. The right hand strikes the duplicate ring against the wand, palming the ring in that action. The left whips away, spinning the original ring on the center of the wand.

11. NEW RING ON WAND

It would be impossible to improve the "Ring on Wand" as done by competent performers, but this version brings it within the range of those whose skill is more limited.

Instead of a ring, a large coin or small disk is used, with a hole in the center slightly greater than the diameter of the wand. This disk is not so innocent as it appears. It is provided with a loose-fitting "shell" which exactly resembles the disk, as long as the proper side of the shell is kept upward.

The magician drops disk and shell as one, down over the wand from the right hand to the left, which is holding the center of the wand in a loose fist. Dipping down into the left fist, the right fingers apparently bring up the disk again, but actually it is left there and the shell alone withdrawn.

Simultaneously the left fist closes over the disk to hide it. To simplify the trick further, the right hand lays the shell aside and throws a cloth over the left, which extends the wand horizontally for someone to take the ends. The left hand is then withdrawn, leaving the disk on the wand beneath the cloth.

The right hand picks up the supposed disk (actually the shell) and pretends to place it in the left hand, really palming it. The left hand goes beneath the cloth and spins the disk already on the wand, while the right whisks away the handkerchief and pockets it, the shell going with it.

12. PASSE PASSE BOTTLES

An old trick with a neat twist. The performer lifts two metal cylinders; under one he shows a quart bottle, under the other a glass. He replaces the covers, recites the words "Passe, Passe," and when he lifts the cylinders the bottle and glass have changed places.

This is repeated, bottle and glass traveling back and forth as often as required. At the finish the magician shows both tubes empty and pours liquid from the bottle into the glass.

Actually there are two bottles and two glasses. The bottles are bottomless so a glass is concealed beneath each. By inserting his forefinger down into a tube, the magician engages a "bottle" so he can lift it and show the glass instead. This accounts for the passage back and forth.

One bottle contains a compartment just below the neck, and this is filled with liquid so it can be poured at the finish. The other bottle is slightly larger and is an absolute shell. Just before the climax the magician casually switches cylinders, so he places the "shell" bottle over the one containing the liquid. The two bottles then appear as one, enabling the magician to show both tubes empty.

Both bottles have holes in the back, so by lining them up the magician can insert a finger, thus pressing the hidden glass against the inside of the bottles while he pours the liquid into the other glass.

Now for an improvement that makes this trick terrific. Just before the climax, an assistant sidles up while the magician is looking elsewhere and reaches down in the tube where the bottle is supposed to be. He pulls out the bottle and sneaks away with it.

The magician gets back to business, saying he will "pass" the bottle to the other tube and back again. The audience is hysterical by the time he lifts the tube from which the assistant "stole" the bottle, because they know it can't possibly be there. But there it is, big as ever, and the magician blandly proceeds as though nothing at all had happened.

The secret is simply an extra "shell" bottle, which is set over the smaller bottle before the trick starts. The magician handles them both as one until the assistant "steals" the shell by drawing it up out of the tube without disturbing the inner bottle. The usual finish follows.

Preferably the master of ceremonies, a comedian, or a skeptical stooge from the audience should be delegated to work the bottle steal, rather than one of the magician's own assistants.

A PERSONAL WORD FROM MELVIN POWERS, PUBLISHER, WILSHIRE BOOK COMPANY

My goal is to publish interesting, informative, and inspirational books. You can help me to accomplish this by sending me your answers to the following questions:

Did you enjoy reading this book? Why?

What ideas in the book impressed you most? Have you applied them to your daily life? How?

Is there a chapter that could serve as a theme for an entire book? Explain.

Would you like to read similar books? What additional information would you like them to contain?

If you have an idea for a book, I would welcome discussing it with you. If you have a manuscript in progress, write or call me concerning possible publication.

Melvin Powers
12015 Sherman Road
North Hollywood, California 91605

(818) 765-8579

MELVIN POWERS SELF-IMPROVEMENT LIBRARY

ASTROLOGY
ASTROLOGY: HOW TO CHART YOUR HOROSCOPE *Max Heindel*	5.00
ASTROLOGY AND SEXUAL ANALYSIS *Morris C. Goodman*	7.00
ASTROLOGY AND YOU *Carroll Righter*	5.00
ASTROLOGY MADE EASY *Astarte*	7.00
ASTROLOGY, ROMANCE, YOU AND THE STARS *Anthony Norvell*	5.00
MY WORLD OF ASTROLOGY *Sydney Omarr*	7.00
THOUGHT DIAL *Sydney Omarr*	7.00
WHAT THE STARS REVEAL ABOUT THE MEN IN YOUR LIFE *Thelma White*	3.00

BRIDGE
BRIDGE BIDDING MADE EASY *Edwin B. Kantar*	10.00
BRIDGE CONVENTIONS *Edwin B. Kantar*	10.00
COMPETITIVE BIDDING IN MODERN BRIDGE *Edgar Kaplan*	7.00
DEFENSIVE BRIDGE PLAY COMPLETE *Edwin B. Kantar*	20.00
GAMESMAN BRIDGE—PLAY BETTER WITH KANTAR *Edwin B. Kantar*	7.00
HOW TO IMPROVE YOUR BRIDGE *Alfred Sheinwold*	7.00
IMPROVING YOUR BIDDING SKILLS *Edwin B. Kantar*	7.00
INTRODUCTION TO DECLARER'S PLAY *Edwin B. Kantar*	7.00
INTRODUCTION TO DEFENDER'S PLAY *Edwin B. Kantar*	7.00
KANTAR FOR THE DEFENSE *Edwin B. Kantar*	7.00
KANTAR FOR THE DEFENSE VOLUME 2 *Edwin B. Kantar*	7.00
TEST YOUR BRIDGE PLAY *Edwin B. Kantar*	7.00
VOLUME 2—TEST YOUR BRIDGE PLAY *Edwin B. Kantar*	10.00
WINNING DECLARER PLAY *Dorothy Hayden Truscott*	10.00

BUSINESS, STUDY & REFERENCE
BRAINSTORMING *Charles Clark*	10.00
CONVERSATION MADE EASY *Elliot Russell*	5.00
EXAM SECRET *Dennis B. Jackson*	5.00
FIX-IT BOOK *Arthur Symons*	2.00
HOW TO DEVELOP A BETTER SPEAKING VOICE *M. Hellier*	5.00
HOW TO SAVE 50% ON GAS & CAR EXPENSES *Ken Stansbie*	5.00
HOW TO SELF-PUBLISH YOUR BOOK & MAKE IT A BEST SELLER *Melvin Powers*	20.00
INCREASE YOUR LEARNING POWER *Geoffrey A. Dudley*	5.00
PRACTICAL GUIDE TO BETTER CONCENTRATION *Melvin Powers*	5.00
7 DAYS TO FASTER READING *William S. Schaill*	7.00
SONGWRITERS' RHYMING DICTIONARY *Jane Shaw Whitfield*	10.00
SPELLING MADE EASY *Lester D. Basch & Dr. Milton Finkelstein*	3.00
STUDENT'S GUIDE TO BETTER GRADES *J. A. Rickard*	3.00
TEST YOURSELF—FIND YOUR HIDDEN TALENT *Jack Shafer*	3.00
YOUR WILL & WHAT TO DO ABOUT IT *Attorney Samuel G. Kling*	7.00

CALLIGRAPHY
ADVANCED CALLIGRAPHY *Katherine Jeffares*	7.00
CALLIGRAPHY—THE ART OF BEAUTIFUL WRITING *Katherine Jeffares*	7.00
CALLIGRAPHY FOR FUN & PROFIT *Anne Leptich & Jacque Evans*	7.00
CALLIGRAPHY MADE EASY *Tina Serafini*	7.00

CHESS & CHECKERS
BEGINNER'S GUIDE TO WINNING CHESS *Fred Reinfeld*	7.00
CHESS IN TEN EASY LESSONS *Larry Evans*	10.00
CHESS MADE EASY *Milton L. Hanauer*	5.00
CHESS PROBLEMS FOR BEGINNERS *Edited by Fred Reinfeld*	5.00
CHESS TACTICS FOR BEGINNERS *Edited by Fred Reinfeld*	7.00

___ HOW TO WIN AT CHECKERS *Fred Reinfeld*	5.00
___ 1001 BRILLIANT WAYS TO CHECKMATE *Fred Reinfeld*	10.00
___ 1001 WINNING CHESS SACRIFICES & COMBINATIONS *Fred Reinfeld*	10.00

COOKERY & HERBS

___ CULPEPER'S HERBAL REMEDIES *Dr. Nicholas Culpeper*	5.00
___ FAST GOURMET COOKBOOK *Poppy Cannon*	2.50
___ HEALING POWER OF HERBS *May Bethel*	5.00
___ HEALING POWER OF NATURAL FOODS *May Bethel*	7.00
___ HERBS FOR HEALTH—HOW TO GROW & USE THEM *Louise Evans Doole*	5.00
___ HOME GARDEN COOKBOOK—DELICIOUS NATURAL FOOD RECIPES *Ken Kraft*	3.00
___ MEATLESS MEAL GUIDE *Tomi Ryan & James H. Ryan, M.D.*	4.00
___ VEGETABLE GARDENING FOR BEGINNERS *Hugh Wiberg*	2.00
___ VEGETABLES FOR TODAY'S GARDENS *R. Milton Carleton*	2.00
___ VEGETARIAN COOKERY *Janet Walker*	7.00
___ VEGETARIAN COOKING MADE EASY & DELECTABLE *Veronica Vezza*	3.00
___ VEGETARIAN DELIGHTS—A HAPPY COOKBOOK FOR HEALTH *K. R. Mehta*	2.00

GAMBLING & POKER

___ HOW TO WIN AT DICE GAMES *Skip Frey*	3.00
___ HOW TO WIN AT POKER *Terence Reese & Anthony T. Watkins*	7.00
___ SCARNE ON DICE *John Scarne*	15.00
___ WINNING AT CRAPS *Dr. Lloyd T. Commins*	5.00
___ WINNING AT GIN *Chester Wander & Cy Rice*	3.00
___ WINNING AT POKER—AN EXPERT'S GUIDE *John Archer*	10.00
___ WINNING AT 21—AN EXPERT'S GUIDE *John Archer*	7.00
___ WINNING POKER SYSTEMS *Norman Zadeh*	3.00

HEALTH

___ BEE POLLEN *Lynda Lyngheim & Jack Scagnetti*	5.00
___ COPING WITH ALZHEIMER'S *Rose Oliver, Ph.D. & Francis Bock, Ph.D.*	10.00
___ DR. LINDNER'S POINT SYSTEM FOOD PROGRAM *Peter G. Lindner, M.D.*	2.00
___ HELP YOURSELF TO BETTER SIGHT *Margaret Darst Corbett*	7.00
___ HOW YOU CAN STOP SMOKING PERMANENTLY *Ernest Caldwell*	5.00
___ MIND OVER PLATTER *Peter G. Lindner, M.D.*	5.00
___ NATURE'S WAY TO NUTRITION & VIBRANT HEALTH *Robert J. Scrutton*	3.00
___ NEW CARBOHYDRATE DIET COUNTER *Patti Lopez-Pereira*	2.00
___ REFLEXOLOGY *Dr. Maybelle Segal*	5.00
___ REFLEXOLOGY FOR GOOD HEALTH *Anna Kaye & Don C. Matchan*	7.00
___ 30 DAYS TO BEAUTIFUL LEGS *Dr. Marc Selner*	3.00
___ WONDER WITHIN *Thomas F. Coyle, M.D.*	10.00
___ YOU CAN LEARN TO RELAX *Dr. Samuel Gutwirth*	5.00

HOBBIES

___ BEACHCOMBING FOR BEGINNERS *Norman Hickin*	2.00
___ BLACKSTONE'S MODERN CARD TRICKS *Harry Blackstone*	7.00
___ BLACKSTONE'S SECRETS OF MAGIC *Harry Blackstone*	7.00
___ COIN COLLECTING FOR BEGINNERS *Burton Hobson & Fred Reinfeld*	7.00
___ ENTERTAINING WITH ESP *Tony 'Doc' Shiels*	2.00
___ 400 FASCINATING MAGIC TRICKS YOU CAN DO *Howard Thurston*	7.00
___ HOW I TURN JUNK INTO FUN AND PROFIT *Sari*	3.00
___ HOW TO WRITE A HIT SONG & SELL IT *Tommy Boyce*	10.00
___ MAGIC FOR ALL AGES *Walter Gibson*	7.00
___ STAMP COLLECTING FOR BEGINNERS *Burton Hobson*	3.00

HORSE PLAYER'S WINNING GUIDES

___ BETTING HORSES TO WIN *Les Conklin*	7.00
___ ELIMINATE THE LOSERS *Bob McKnight*	5.00
___ HOW TO PICK WINNING HORSES *Bob McKnight*	5.00

_ HOW TO WIN AT THE RACES *Sam (The Genius) Lewin*	5.00
_ HOW YOU CAN BEAT THE RACES *Jack Kavanaqh*	5.00
_ MAKING MONEY AT THE RACES *David Barr*	5.00
_ PAYDAY AT THE RACES *Les Conklin*	7.00
_ SMART HANDICAPPING MADE EASY *William Bauman*	5.00
_ SUCCESS AT THE HARNESS RACES *Barry Meadow*	7.00

HUMOR

_ HOW TO FLATTEN YOUR TUSH *Coach Marge Reardon*	2.00
_ JOKE TELLER'S HANDBOOK *Bob Orben*	7.00
_ JOKES FOR ALL OCCASIONS *Al Schock*	5.00
_ 2,000 NEW LAUGHS FOR SPEAKERS *Bob Orben*	7.00
_ 2,400 JOKES TO BRIGHTEN YOUR SPEECHES *Robert Orben*	7.00
_ 2,500 JOKES TO START 'EM LAUGHING *Bob Orben*	10.00

HYPNOTISM

_ CHILDBIRTH WITH HYPNOSIS *William S. Kroger, M.D.*	5.00
_ HOW TO SOLVE YOUR SEX PROBLEMS WITH SELF-HYPNOSIS *Frank S. Caprio, M.D.*	5.00
_ HOW TO STOP SMOKING THRU SELF-HYPNOSIS *Leslie M. LeCron*	3.00
_ HOW YOU CAN BOWL BETTER USING SELF-HYPNOSIS *Jack Heise*	7.00
_ HOW YOU CAN PLAY BETTER GOLF USING SELF-HYPNOSIS *Jack Heise*	3.00
_ HYPNOSIS AND SELF-HYPNOSIS *Bernard Hollander, M.D.*	7.00
_ HYPNOTISM *(Originally published in 1893) Carl Sextus*	5.00
_ HYPNOTISM MADE EASY *Dr. Ralph Winn*	7.00
_ HYPNOTISM MADE PRACTICAL *Louis Orton*	5.00
_ HYPNOTISM REVEALED *Melvin Powers*	3.00
_ HYPNOTISM TODAY *Leslie LeCron and Jean Bordeaux, Ph.D.*	5.00
_ MODERN HYPNOSIS *Lesley Kuhn & Salvatore Russo, Ph.D.*	5.00
_ NEW CONCEPTS OF HYPNOSIS *Bernard C. Gindes, M.D.*	10.00
_ NEW SELF-HYPNOSIS *Paul Adams*	10.00
_ POST-HYPNOTIC INSTRUCTIONS—SUGGESTIONS FOR THERAPY *Arnold Furst*	10.00
_ PRACTICAL GUIDE TO SELF-HYPNOSIS *Melvin Powers*	5.00
_ PRACTICAL HYPNOTISM *Philip Magonet, M.D.*	3.00
_ SECRETS OF HYPNOTISM *S. J. Van Pelt, M.D.*	5.00
_ SELF-HYPNOSIS—A CONDITIONED-RESPONSE TECHNIQUE *Laurence Sparks*	7.00
_ SELF-HYPNOSIS—ITS THEORY, TECHNIQUE & APPLICATION *Melvin Powers*	3.00
_ THERAPY THROUGH HYPNOSIS *Edited by Raphael H. Rhodes*	5.00

JUDAICA

_ SERVICE OF THE HEART *Evelyn Garfiel, Ph.D.*	10.00
_ STORY OF ISRAEL IN COINS *Jean & Maurice Gould*	2.00
_ STORY OF ISRAEL IN STAMPS *Maxim & Gabriel Shamir*	1.00
_ TONGUE OF THE PROPHETS *Robert St. John*	10.00

JUST FOR WOMEN

_ COSMOPOLITAN'S GUIDE TO MARVELOUS MEN *Foreword by Helen Gurley Brown*	3.00
_ COSMOPOLITAN'S HANG-UP HANDBOOK *Foreword by Helen Gurley Brown*	4.00
_ COSMOPOLITAN'S LOVE BOOK—A GUIDE TO ECSTASY IN BED	7.00
_ COSMOPOLITAN'S NEW ETIQUETTE GUIDE *Foreword by Helen Gurley Brown*	4.00
_ I AM A COMPLEAT WOMAN *Doris Hagopian & Karen O'Connor Sweeney*	3.00
_ JUST FOR WOMEN—A GUIDE TO THE FEMALE BODY *Richard E. Sand, M.D.*	5.00
_ NEW APPROACHES TO SEX IN MARRIAGE *John E. Eichenlaub, M.D.*	3.00
_ SEXUALLY ADEQUATE FEMALE *Frank S. Caprio, M.D.*	3.00
_ SEXUALLY FULFILLED WOMAN *Dr. Rachel Copelan*	5.00

MARRIAGE, SEX & PARENTHOOD

___ ABILITY TO LOVE *Dr. Allan Fromme*	7.00
___ GUIDE TO SUCCESSFUL MARRIAGE *Drs. Albert Ellis & Robert Harper*	7.00
___ HOW TO RAISE AN EMOTIONALLY HEALTHY, HAPPY CHILD *Albert Ellis, Ph.D.*	10.00
___ PARENT SURVIVAL TRAINING *Marvin Silverman, Ed.D. & David Lustig, Ph.D.*	10.00
___ SEX WITHOUT GUILT *Albert Ellis, Ph.D.*	7.00
___ SEXUALLY ADEQUATE MALE *Frank S. Caprio, M.D.*	3.00
___ SEXUALLY FULFILLED MAN *Dr. Rachel Copelan*	5.00
___ STAYING IN LOVE *Dr. Norton F. Kristy*	7.00

MELVIN POWERS' MAIL ORDER LIBRARY

___ HOW TO GET RICH IN MAIL ORDER *Melvin Powers*	20.00
___ HOW TO SELF-PUBLISH YOUR BOOK & MAKE IT A BEST SELLER *Melvin Powers*	20.00
___ HOW TO WRITE A GOOD ADVERTISEMENT *Victor O. Schwab*	20.00
___ MAIL ORDER MADE EASY *J. Frank Brumbaugh*	20.00

METAPHYSICS & OCCULT

___ CONCENTRATION—A GUIDE TO MENTAL MASTERY *Mouni Sadhu*	7.00
___ EXTRA-TERRESTRIAL INTELLIGENCE—THE FIRST ENCOUNTER	6.00
___ FORTUNE TELLING WITH CARDS *P. Foli*	5.00
___ HOW TO INTERPRET DREAMS, OMENS & FORTUNE TELLING SIGNS *Gettings*	5.00
___ HOW TO UNDERSTAND YOUR DREAMS *Geoffrey A. Dudley*	5.00
___ IN DAYS OF GREAT PEACE *Mouni Sadhu*	3.00
___ MAGICIAN—HIS TRAINING AND WORK *W. E. Butler*	7.00
___ MEDITATION *Mouni Sadhu*	10.00
___ MODERN NUMEROLOGY *Morris C. Goodman*	5.00
___ NUMEROLOGY—ITS FACTS AND SECRETS *Ariel Yvon Taylor*	5.00
___ NUMEROLOGY MADE EASY *W. Mykian*	5.00
___ PALMISTRY MADE EASY *Fred Gettings*	5.00
___ PALMISTRY MADE PRACTICAL *Elizabeth Daniels Squire*	7.00
___ PROPHECY IN OUR TIME *Martin Ebon*	2.50
___ SUPERSTITION—ARE YOU SUPERSTITIOUS? *Eric Maple*	2.00
___ TAROT *Mouni Sadhu*	10.00
___ TAROT OF THE BOHEMIANS *Papus*	7.00
___ WAYS TO SELF-REALIZATION *Mouni Sadhu*	7.00
___ WITCHCRAFT, MAGIC & OCCULTISM—A FASCINATING HISTORY *W. B. Crow*	10.00
___ WITCHCRAFT—THE SIXTH SENSE *Justine Glass*	7.00

RECOVERY

___ KNIGHT IN RUSTY ARMOR *Robert Fisher*	5.00
___ KNIGHT IN RUSTY ARMOR *Robert Fisher (Hard cover edition)*	10.00

SELF-HELP & INSPIRATIONAL

___ CHARISMA—HOW TO GET "THAT SPECIAL MAGIC" *Marcia Grad*	7.00
___ DAILY POWER FOR JOYFUL LIVING *Dr. Donald Curtis*	7.00
___ DYNAMIC THINKING *Melvin Powers*	5.00
___ GREATEST POWER IN THE UNIVERSE *U. S. Andersen*	7.00
___ GROW RICH WHILE YOU SLEEP *Ben Sweetland*	8.00
___ GROW RICH WITH YOUR MILLION DOLLAR MIND *Brian Adams*	7.00
___ GROWTH THROUGH REASON *Albert Ellis, Ph.D.*	10.00
___ GUIDE TO PERSONAL HAPPINESS *Albert Ellis, Ph.D. & Irving Becker, Ed.D.*	10.00
___ HANDWRITING ANALYSIS MADE EASY *John Marley*	7.00
___ HANDWRITING TELLS *Nadya Olyanova*	7.00
___ HOW TO ATTRACT GOOD LUCK *A.H.Z. Carr*	7.00
___ HOW TO DEVELOP A WINNING PERSONALITY *Martin Panzer*	7.00
___ HOW TO DEVELOP AN EXCEPTIONAL MEMORY *Young & Gibson*	7.00
___ HOW TO LIVE WITH A NEUROTIC *Albert Ellis, Ph.D.*	7.00
___ HOW TO OVERCOME YOUR FEARS *M. P. Leahy, M.D.*	3.00
___ HOW TO SUCCEED *Brian Adams*	7.00

HUMAN PROBLEMS & HOW TO SOLVE THEM *Dr. Donald Curtis*	5.00
I CAN *Ben Sweetland*	8.00
I WILL *Ben Sweetland*	8.00
KNIGHT IN RUSTY ARMOR *Robert Fisher*	5.00
KNIGHT IN RUSTY ARMOR *Robert Fisher (Hard cover edition)*	10.00
LEFT-HANDED PEOPLE *Michael Barsley*	5.00
MAGIC IN YOUR MIND *U.S. Andersen*	10.00
MAGIC OF THINKING SUCCESS *Dr. David J. Schwartz*	8.00
MAGIC POWER OF YOUR MIND *Walter M. Germain*	7.00
MENTAL POWER THROUGH SLEEP SUGGESTION *Melvin Powers*	3.00
NEVER UNDERESTIMATE THE SELLING POWER OF A WOMAN *Dottie Walters*	7.00
NEW GUIDE TO RATIONAL LIVING *Albert Ellis, Ph.D. & R. Harper, Ph.D.*	10.00
PSYCHO-CYBERNETICS *Maxwell Maltz, M.D.*	7.00
PSYCHOLOGY OF HANDWRITING *Nadya Olyanova*	7.00
SALES CYBERNETICS *Brian Adams*	10.00
SCIENCE OF MIND IN DAILY LIVING *Dr. Donald Curtis*	7.00
SECRET OF SECRETS *U.S. Andersen*	7.00
SECRET POWER OF THE PYRAMIDS *U. S. Andersen*	7.00
SELF-THERAPY FOR THE STUTTERER *Malcolm Frazer*	3.00
SUCCESS-CYBERNETICS *U. S. Andersen*	7.00
10 DAYS TO A GREAT NEW LIFE *William E. Edwards*	3.00
THINK AND GROW RICH *Napoleon Hill*	8.00
THINK LIKE A WINNER *Dr. Walter Doyle Staples*	10.00
THREE MAGIC WORDS *U. S. Andersen*	10.00
TREASURY OF COMFORT *Edited by Rabbi Sidney Greenberg*	10.00
TREASURY OF THE ART OF LIVING *Sidney S. Greenberg*	7.00
WHAT YOUR HANDWRITING REVEALS *Albert E. Hughes*	4.00
WONDER WITHIN *Thomas F. Coyle, M.D.*	10.00
YOUR SUBCONSCIOUS POWER *Charles M. Simmons*	7.00
YOUR THOUGHTS CAN CHANGE YOUR LIFE *Dr. Donald Curtis*	7.00

SPORTS

BILLIARDS—POCKET • CAROM • THREE CUSHION *Clive Cottingham, Jr.*	7.00
COMPLETE GUIDE TO FISHING *Vlad Evanoff*	2.00
HOW TO IMPROVE YOUR RACQUETBALL *Lubarsky, Kaufman & Scagnetti*	5.00
HOW TO WIN AT POCKET BILLIARDS *Edward D. Knuchell*	10.00
JOY OF WALKING *Jack Scagnetti*	3.00
LEARNING & TEACHING SOCCER SKILLS *Eric Worthington*	3.00
RACQUETBALL FOR WOMEN *Toni Hudson, Jack Scagnetti & Vince Rondone*	3.00
SECRET OF BOWLING STRIKES *Dawson Taylor*	5.00
SOCCER—THE GAME & HOW TO PLAY IT *Gary Rosenthal*	7.00
STARTING SOCCER *Edward F. Dolan, Jr.*	3.00

TENNIS LOVER'S LIBRARY

HOW TO BEAT BETTER TENNIS PLAYERS *Loring Fiske*	4.00
PSYCH YOURSELF TO BETTER TENNIS *Dr. Walter A. Luszki*	2.00
TENNIS FOR BEGINNERS *Dr. H. A. Murray*	2.00
TENNIS MADE EASY *Joel Brecheen*	5.00
WEEKEND TENNIS—HOW TO HAVE FUN & WIN AT THE SAME TIME *Bill Talbert*	3.00

WILSHIRE PET LIBRARY

DOG TRAINING MADE EASY & FUN *John W. Kellogg*	5.00
HOW TO BRING UP YOUR PET DOG *Kurt Unkelbach*	2.00
HOW TO RAISE & TRAIN YOUR PUPPY *Jeff Griffen*	5.00

books listed above can be obtained from your book dealer or directly from Melvin Powers.
ordering, please remit $2.00 postage for the first book and $1.00 for each additional book.

Melvin Powers
12015 Sherman Road, No. Hollywood, California 91605

WILSHIRE HORSE LOVERS' LIBRARY

Notes

Notes

Notes